DATE

TEACHERS COLLEGE
STUDIES IN EDUCATION

RECENT TITLES

THE CLASH

OF CULTURES

IN ISRAEL

A Problem for Education

ABRAHAM SHUMSKY, Ed. D.

THE SCHOOL OF EDUCATION
THE CITY COLLEGE OF THE CITY OF NEW YORK

Bureau of Publications

TEACHERS COLLEGE, COLUMBIA UNIVERSITY

NEW YORK, 1955

TO MY FATHER

SHMUEL

AND MY MOTHER

ADELA

אל מול הרך התאחדנו,
יושיט ידו אח אל אח.

We Were United Before Your Mountains,
Brother to Brother, Hand to Hand.

S. TCHERNIKHOVSKY

In Acknowledgment

This study was written as a doctoral dissertation at Teachers College, Columbia University. I want to express particular appreciation to the members of my doctoral committee—Professors Alice Miel, Stephen M. Corey, and Goodwin Watson—for their warm encouragement and constructive criticism.

In working on the project I learned much from the writings of three Israeli scholars and students of the Israeli ethnic problem: Dr. S. N. Eisenstadt, Dr. C. Frankenstein, and Mr. I. Yeshayahu. My study is based on their pioneering and scientific work.

A. S.

Contents

Part Four

THE ETHNIC PROBLEM AND THE SCHOOL

Part Five

SUMMARY

Part One

INTRODUCTION

I

Introduction

Evidence of Ethnic Group Conflict and
Tension in Israel

A DISTINGUISHED ISRAELI WHO AFTER A LONG ABSENCE HAD
returned to Israel for the holidays was heard to remark, after listening
to some of his countrymen: "A silent film about Israel right now would
be wonderful; but if you were to put in sound, it would be ruined! The
accomplishments you can see are fine—new settlements, new roads, new
factories—but what you hear is not so good. . . ."

This is as much as to say that, difficult as are Israel's material problems, they are not so harrowing as her moral and psychological problems.

These problems are very largely those involved in the basic task of
integrating the cultures of widely disparate elements, whose only common
bond appears to be that they are Jewish.

The Jewish community in Israel consists of two main groups. One
group is composed of those whose forebears settled in Europe, in the
Diaspora, and who are called Ashkenazi; the other is composed of those
whose cultural setting is in the Middle and Far East and the Mediter-
ranean region and who are called Oriental. While there are differences
amongst the people coming from different European countries, it is
on the whole correct to assume that the majority have an understanding
of the social implications of modern industrial civilization. The Orientals, on the other hand, are characterized on the whole by passivity and
by limited technological knowledge resulting from centuries of life in
the feudal Orient. The contact between these two cultures has resulted

3

in some problems, tensions, and conflicts. A brief survey of the Oriental and Ashkenazi views of the situation, and of "incidents" to which it has given rise, will provide a perspective for the study of the problems.

THE ORIENTAL VIEW

An Indian-Jewish philosopher views the conflict as a clash between two philosophies of life—that of Western civilization, as represented by the Ashkenazi Jewry, and that of Eastern civilization, as represented by the Oriental Jewry:

> The idea that the Jewish state constitutes a "melting pot" for all the multifarious cultural forces is indeed a magnificent idea; but we cannot see that the Western cultures in Israel are in a process of melting. The belief that Western culture and civilization are, after all, superior to the "lethargic" and "drowsy" civilization of the East is still accepted by many thinking Israelis. In the European view social life is intrinsic with economic and material aspirations. For the Indian, on the other hand, bread and butter are certainly necessary, but one's conscious relation to God creates a sense of personal and social responsibility which the European can scarcely comprehend. . . . We fear the loss of all that has been dear to us. (M1:4)*

In 1952, Israel Yeshayahu, a prominent Yemenite leader, described the ethnic group tension in an article which has become a center of controversy. He feels that during the last few years there has been evidence of increasing ethnic aggressiveness on the part of the Ashkenazi Jewry. This aggressiveness, he says, is not felt among the leaders but is quite conspicuous among the general public, and is motivated by "a racial instinct of survival" which makes itself felt as fear of becoming a minority in Israel. This fear is rationalized into the thesis that if the Orientals ever become a majority, all the achievements of organized labor and Western civilization may be wiped out or at least considerably weakened.

Mr. Yeshayahu expresses his feelings frankly:

> I respect the ability, culture, enterprise and generosity of the Ashkenazi Jewry, and especially what they have given us Orientals. But all this was philanthropy and charity. And it is not easy or pleasant to

---

* Symbols in parentheses refer to Bibliography items, each of which has a letter-number designation (B1, Y4, etc.). A number separated from this designation by a colon is the page number. (M1:4, for instance, means reference M1, page 4.)

receive charity and to be dependent on others: dependency is not a healthy framework for relations of equality and friendship. (Y4:4)

The ethnic group tension is especially strong among the new immigrants. Many of them interpret unsatisfactory living conditions as ethnic discrimination. In an interview, a Moroccan Jew said:

"This country is good, but its people are bad, they don't give us what we need; we are like unloved stepchildren; every immigrant who does not know Yiddish [a language spoken by the Ashkenazim but not spoken by the Orientals] does not count. . . . The government and the officials are all Yiddish, and are all bad." (E4:138)

They point out that the overwhelming majority of the officials are Ashkenazim and say that it is difficult to get ahead without having a relative or a friend in the government. The behavior of the officials is criticized as being characterized by attitudes of superiority, social distance, and unreadiness to give and take: "The Ashkenazim do not want to live with us; we are for them like a herd; they only want our votes for their politics." (E4:158)

The Orientals resent the fact of belonging as a group to the lower-class strata, and feel that heavy barriers separate the socio-economic classes. "They are all masters—they have houses, good jobs, and positions—and we are only servants for them; they are so proud—and they want to rule us and force us to remain in this inferior position." (E4:150)

A most critical issue is the fact that the Orientals are not represented sufficiently in the local and central government organs. For instance, in April 1952 there were only six Orientals among the 120 members of the parliament although the Oriental group constituted more than a third of the population. (A4:13)

THE ASHKENAZI VIEW

The Ashkenazi group assumes that the Oriental community should be absorbed by the Western culture. They are appalled by what they see as the low standard of achievement and sloppy work habits of many Orientals. They never tire of pointing out that before the last war you could leave your house, or barn, or car, unlocked without fear, whereas now the police can scarcely cope with the volume of petty larceny. "What is going to happen?" the old-timer Ashkenazi asks. "Is this country going to become an Oriental slum?"

An editorial in the liberal newspaper *Haaretz* says:

The bringing of too many people from underdeveloped countries may constitute a threat to the existence of the Israeli state. . . . Unity of origin is not sufficient for creating national unity, when one part of the nation is socially and culturally underdeveloped. . . . The Zionist movement is faced with an unforeseen task: bringing Western culture to Oriental Jewry. (H1:2)

The Minister of Education sees the problem of social integration as the major task of education. In a 1952 address he pointed out that it is a question now of another type of Jewry—one that does not know the Western value system, one that was not nurtured by the rich streams of Western Jewish life: the Hasidut ("piety"), Haskala (Enlightenment), and Emancipation movements, modern Hebrew literature, the Labor and Agricultural movements. Integration, then, means bridging the gap between two worlds.

Speaking about prejudice, the Minister warned:

When one overhears expressions about the "dark Jews," it is difficult not to be pessimistic about the fate of our nation . . . There is a danger that gradually we are going to consist of two different nations. (D5:5)

The Israeli population is united in the conviction that every effort has to be made to create national unity. There is encouraging evidence of many successes in acculturation, mainly through cooperative living and education. But in spite of this national aspiration and ideology, and in spite of the Ashkenazim's claim that there is no discrimination in Israel, one can sense attitudes of prejudice towards the Oriental Jew. The prejudice is expressed in "stereotyping" and in connecting ethnic groups with various characteristics: dirtiness, noisiness, aggressiveness, mental inferiority, shrewdness, and so forth.

An anonymous writer expressed his feelings on this matter in a letter to an American Jewish leader who is associated with the Immigration Department. He stated that the old-timer Ashkenazim are really terribly concerned and "full of anxiety" about the new Oriental immigrants.

. . . they definitely are not my kith and kin—they are not worse, but they are different, and I don't want to have them slowly becoming (as they are) the dominant feature of this country, there being no white balance to their influx. (S2:8)

In a visit to a local government office in Tel Aviv, this letter-writer saw Oriental girls working as apprentices, and felt, so he says, as if he were in a zoo. He then recalls a well-known incident of the immigrant camps during the recent floods:

> It was the most grotesque and disheartening sight in the world. Their Oriental inmates not only refused to move a finger in order to help the volunteers who came to evacuate them; they stood in circles around those who were carrying their scanty belongings, and clapped their hands and sang: "Stupid Ashkenazi, stupid . . ." (S2:8)

He claims that all the clothing amassed throughout the country for the Oriental immigrants was found two days later all over Tel Aviv—sold "by your black darlings, on the black market." (S2:9) Finally, he also mentions the economic crisis in the country, and the resulting low level of morale and its impact on the absorption of immigrants:

> You must understand how we feel. Lately we are all of us, even the sweetest tempered of my kind, at the end of our nervous tether. Life is terribly hard—one cannot live and work and be healthy on rations. Your "ingathered" African exiles probably manage very well, but we cannot. (S2:9)

It is difficult to generalize and say how much this anonymous letter represents the feelings of the Ashkenazi community, because there are not sufficient data on this issue. A research institution which attempted to study the intercommunal attitudes failed to get the cooperation of the public: "Many refrained from answering our questions, because in our society there is a negative attitude towards the individual who expresses feelings of prejudice." (I1:22) But the general impression is that many of the Ashkenazim look on the Oriental group often with feelings of superiority or contempt, perhaps with pity, strangeness, or some fear, but seldom with brotherly respect. (F6)

ETHNIC TENSION AND "INCIDENTS"

The accumulation of tension is very explosive and dangerous. During the last three years, it has developed in a few instances into attacks and clashes. The most famous incident occurred in the village of Tel-Mond, where an Iraqi leader was killed in an accident. The Iraqi group (living in a camp near the village) interpreted the accident as "a murder of our brother by the Ashkenazim" and stormed the village, shouting, "Slaughter the Ashkenazim!" Only the immediate intervention of a strong police force prevented the situation from deteriorating into a bloody fight.

It was the purpose of this section, not to survey and analyze the ethnic group problem in Israel, but only to show some evidence of the existence of ethnic group conflict and tension in this young country.

The general feeling of the public is that the improvement of ethnic group relations is a major task confronting the new state.

The Study

The purposes, procedures, and limitations of the study are listed, and certain often used terms defined, in the following outline:

PURPOSES

1. To analyze the impact of ethnic group contacts and tension on the Israeli child (mainly the Oriental Jewish child), with emphasis on the manifestations and consequences of this impact in the school.
2. To suggest ways and illustrate programs by which the school can improve ethnic group relationships.
3. To review the major writings and research on this question.
4. To suggest further research.

PROCEDURES

1. Survey of the Israeli literature dealing with the problem.
2. Correspondence with Israeli leaders to gain more information.
3. Description of American school programs dealing with ethnic group relations and consideration of ways of adapting them to conditions in Israel.
4. Application of modern educational and socio-psychological concepts to analysis of Israeli problems.

TERMS

Ethnic groups. There are several Israeli ethnic groups, but in this study the population will be considered as being divided mainly into these two:

1. *Ashkenazim*—Jews whose background is part of Western civilization.
2. *Oriental Jews*—An Israeli term for Jews whose roots are in the Middle and Far East and Africa (except for South Africa), and for the "Spanish" (Sephardic) Jews (from Italy, Turkey, Egypt, and the Balkan countries).

LIMITATIONS

1. Arab-Israel relations will not be discussed.
2. The study will include illustrative, but not systematic, descriptions of the different ethnic groups.
3. General suggestions for the school's role will be derived from elaboration of principles and illustrations of programs, but construction of a systematic and comprehensive curriculum will not be attempted.

Part Two

CULTURE CONTACT IN ISRAEL

II

The Ashkenazi Community

THE ASHKENAZI JEWS CAME TO ISRAEL FROM ALMOST EVERY country in the Occident. Living in those lands they differed from one another in their way of life. But in Israel, before 1948, these ethnic differences disappeared to a considerable extent in the immigrants' own generation, and entirely among their children. (E9)

In other countries of immigration, like the United States of America, "those groups who come earlier establish themselves in social and economic key positions which give them greater social prestige and a higher standard of living." (E8) Some ethnic groups never achieve complete social and economic equality. Their place in the social and status hierarchy is determined mainly by the time of their immigration, their economic flexibility, and their cultural resemblance to the dominant group. (W2)

In this respect the pattern of Occidental immigration to Israel is unique. Until the establishment of the State, fusion and integration of all these groups from the various countries was manifested in every avenue of people's lives. There is almost complete fusion in political parties and organizations. It is difficult to point out any degree of occupational concentration, or monopoly, on the part of any of those Western groups. There are no social barriers which influence marriages of immigrants from different Western countries, and no different ethnic patterns of educating children. Contact among the various waves of Western immigration was not restricted to formal relations; the newcomers came into close association with the old-timers and were accepted into their primary groups.

13

In short, the various Western groups which arrived in Israel before
1948 merged into a new nation and lost their previous ethnic belongingness and identification. (E8)

This phenomenon of social integration can be understood adequately
only in the light of the motivational forces that brought these various
groups to Israel. "A large segment of the Palestinian community came
there as a result of a conscious negation of Jewish life in the various
lands of the diaspora, and out of the desire to overcome this negation
through the creation of a new society in Palestine." (E9:3)

The end of the nineteenth century was an era of crisis in Jewish life.
As a result of the Haskala (Enlightenment) movement, many of the
European Jews were no longer limited to the traditional patterns of
Jewish culture. On one hand, they felt that the Ghetto life was not ex-
pressing fully the Jewish creative genius and that it was impotent, purposeless, and even degenerate. On the other hand, they were convinced
(especially after the Russian pogroms in 1882) that even the modern
and "emancipated" Jew would not be accepted by the Gentile world.
The banner of "Auto-Emancipation" was raised by Pinsker in 1882 and
paved the way for the Zionist movement. This movement called upon
the Jewish people to immigrate to Palestine and build not only a new
country but also a new culture and nation.

The three major principles of the Zionist ideology were: (1) return
to Palestine, (2) changing of the Jewish occupational structure—from
a nation composed mainly of middlemen to a nation comprising workers, farmers, middlemen, soldiers, professionals, and so forth, and (3)
developing a modern Hebrew culture.

These three principles are interdependent. The poet Bialik expressed
this idea in a symbolic way: "The size of the Sky [symbol of Culture]
above the head of a nation, equals the size of the Earth under their
feet." The conviction was that only with the realization of the first two
principles ("Return" and "Normalization") was a revival of Hebrew
culture possible.

Unlike the American immigration that was motivated mainly by economic drives and characterized by striving for higher and more finan-
cially rewarding positions, the Ashkenazi immigrations emphasized the
normalization of the Jewish occupational structure as a national
goal. (E9)

The rejection of the negative elements in traditional Judaism was an integral part of a cultural transformation that aimed at synthesizing the positive aspects of Judaism and the progressive aspects of modern civilization. The dream was not only to build a Jewish state and nation, but also to establish a model society based on social justice and equality. The abandonment of part of the old exile patterns of living and thinking did not lead to a cultural vacuum (which is so dangerous to the mental health of a society, and especially an immigrant society) because it was accompanied by an active movement of cultural reconstruction. (E9)

The whole Jewish culture was reinterpreted in the light of the Zionist ideology. The old emphasis on the importance of the relationship between the individual and his God was changed into a stress on the importance of the individual's identification with and participation in the task of building a new culture and country. Similarly, the concept of a Messiah changed from a patient and fatalistic expectation of a supernatural power to a concept of dynamic and collective actions by human beings.

The ego-ideal of the community, which for centuries had been the scholar, became personified in a task-oriented individual, the pioneer, whose physical and spiritual energies had to be always mobilized toward the achievement of the national goal—the task.

Yiddish, the language spoken for centuries by Occidental Jews everywhere, was abandoned, and Hebrew became the national language. While the content of Ghetto literature and poetry had emphasized "troubles," praying, and praising God, the Israeli literature and poetry stressed the national concepts of land, water, work, immigration, and defense. The melodies of the old songs were those suggestive of praying and crying (the cantor's music); the new were dynamic, confidence-filling, and martial.

Many of the holidays lost their purely religious character and assumed a secular national character. For instance, Hanuka had been traditionally celebrated for the miracle of the sacred oil which was sufficient to light the Temple's lamps for eight days. In Israel, Hanuka assumed new importance, where the national heroism of the Maccabees, and its contemporary re-emergence, was stressed.

Organized education, in its attempt to create the task-oriented pioneer, stressed these values in the schools. Even the kindergarten rhymes dealt with land and immigration.

These aspirations and motivations, termed by Eisenstadt "the predisposition to change" (E4:21), explain the relative smoothness with which the various Ashkenazi ethnic groups (which arrived in Israel before 1948) were welded.

> Unlike other immigrations, the dissolution of the old traditional life did not result in an *impersonal atomized* society. The dissolution was only one element in the total process of cultural and national transformation, which aimed at the re-creation of a cohesive social and cultural structure. (E8:164)

There were other important factors which contributed toward quick integration. (E8) The Ashkenazi immigration waves were "autoselected" and were composed of small groups of relatively young people. These factors strengthened their readiness to change.

The social and economic conditions in the country itself were conducive to mutual assimilation. Most of the time there was a shortage of manpower. The new immigrants, especially the skilled workers and professionals, were easily absorbed by the *various* branches of the economy and came into close contact with the old-timers.

Since the Jewish community in Palestine lacked state powers, it could perform all the necessary functions of a modern society only through the voluntary democratic organization of its members. A strong public opinion was created, based on the equality of all the ethnic groups and their identification with the national aspirations.

The relentless political struggle for immigration, and especially the heroic movement of "illegal immigration," created an atmosphere conducive to integration, by making immigration a national mission and by raising the self-esteem of the immigrants themselves.

There are three exceptions to the smooth integration of the Ashkenazi groups that immigrated prior to the establishment of the State of Israel:

1. A very small, extremely orthodox Ashkenazi group, called Neturei-Karta ("Guardians of the City"), was not influenced by the new national aspirations, and transplanted Ghetto life to Israel. They remain, even in the present, socially and ecologically isolated.

2. The Jewish immigration from Germany was not integrated as easily as the other groups. At first a degree of social distance and isolation was created, accompanied by some ecological concentration. The feeling of ethnic belongingness and identification in the German

group developed even into an attempt to sustain a new political party—
"The New Immigration." But after a few years, even this wave of immigration integrated with the whole of the Ashkenazi community. It
was not a *passive* absorption, but rather *mutual* assimilation and cultural synthesis. The German immigration changed the Israeli civilization by helping to raise its standard of living, technologically and culturally.

3. Many of the European refugees who arrived *after* the establishment of the new State failed to integrate with the Israeli community
and continued to constitute groups which preserve their ethnic identification, belongingness, and ecological concentration.

The reasons for this non-integration are partly to be found in the
motivational forces that brought these groups to Israel: chiefly in the
hope to find political and economic security and to restore the conditions to which they were accustomed before the Nazi catastrophe—a
factor that created resistance to change. (E4) On the other hand,
changes in the social, economic, and psychological conditions in the new
State itself have made integration a very long and difficult process.

But these failures and difficulties in mutual assimilation are quite
secondary compared with the major issue—the social integration of the
Oriental with the Ashkenazi community.

III

Differences in Motivation

UNDER THE IMPACT OF THE ZIONIST MOVEMENT, THE VARious Western ethnic groups which arrived in Israel before 1948 have merged into a new nation and lost their ethnic belongingness and identification. These processes, however, were not sufficient to unify the Ashkenazi with the Oriental groups.

Five years ago, open discussion of ethnic group tensions and differences was very unpopular and uncommon in Israel. But today the question of ethnic group relations has become a front-page issue. The feeling is widespread that the nation is divided—that there are two Israels: Occidental and Oriental.

This chapter will begin the discussion of the essential differences between these two groups, and the analysis of the major causes underlying their failure to integrate.

Loyalty to the Jewish people, adherence to the Jewish faith, and the aspiration to build a nation undifferentiated according to ethnic groups constitute the common denominator uniting the two communities. This common denominator, however, was found insufficient to carry the aspiration of unity into practice.

There has never been a period in the history of the Jewish people when Jews of Oriental origin did not immigrate to Israel. These waves of immigration, however, did not originate in any national movement aiming at the reconstruction of Jewish life, as did the movement of Zionist liberation. Zionism endeavored to revolutionize the very foundations of the nation's existence; the aim was to change and normalize the Jewish economy, and to revive and secularize the Jewish culture and

18

base it on a synthesis of biblical traditions and modern civilization. The Oriental Jews hardly participated in this social movement. Zionism has never succeeded in ploughing deep furrows among the Jews in the Arab countries. Zionist activities had rarely been noticeable there. "True, these communities had always been imbued with messianic aspirations, and a burning love for Zion and Jerusalem; yet they proved almost disinterested in the problems of the people and the land. They scarcely paid attention to the ways and means of achieving national and social revival." (Z1:2) Says a Yemenite leader: " 'Ashkenazi' and 'Zionist' are overlapping concepts. We also immigrated to Israel, but without being Zionists. Until I came to this country, I knew nothing about the existence of Zionism." (Y4:3)

From time to time efforts were made to reach the Jews in the Arab countries; to awaken them from their lethargy and sow within them the seeds of revolt against their degenerate life in the Diaspora. "However, these attempts never assumed the proportion or met with the success that the movement of Jewish emancipation experienced in Europe." (Z1:4)

About forty years ago, Yavnieli went to Yemen, where he set on foot an immigration movement to Israel. Yavnieli's activities cannot, however, in any way be regarded as a strictly Zionist mission, since Zionism was not interpreted in Yemen as a political and social movement. Yavnieli issued his call for immigration in Messianic terms, covering up the secular and active character of the reconstructing Zionist movement. (Z1) The difference between a Messianic and a Zionist immigration requires more elaboration.

The Hebrew language has two terms for immigrants; one is Olim ("those who go up") and the other is Mehagrim ("immigrants"). These two terms are used interchangeably. Eisenstadt (E6) suggests, however, that from the sociological point of view, the two terms are not identical.

The Olim came to Israel as a result of a conscious negation of some aspects of Jewish life in the Diaspora. Their immigration was motivated by a pioneer urge to build a new way of life. The Mehagrim immigrated not because of conscious rejection of their way of life, but because of economic, religious, or political conditions which compelled them to leave the old country. In the new land they are not interested in building up a new culture, but rather seek to preserve their former way of life and make only the minimum necessary adjustments to the new environment. While the Olim are characterized by a predisposition to change, the Mehagrim are characterized by resistance to change. The Olim are mainly the Ashkenazim who came before 1948; the Mehagrim are mainly the Orientals.

Israel is confronted with the enormous task of welding and integrating these two types of immigrants who differ so much in their motivations for immigrating and consequently in their predispositions toward social change. These differences underlie the failure of the two groups to integrate and join hands in the common task of rebuilding the country and the nation.

It is noteworthy that with the steady rise of modern Israel, the Oriental Jewry has decreased both in numbers and in influence, as compared with the Ashkenazi population. There was a short time at the beginning of the First World War when the Oriental (mainly Sephardi) section of the population approximated in numbers the Ashkenazi section, and even exceeded it. (P2)

Meanwhile, however, the community had been undergoing profound changes. New forms of Jewish life were being established, based on mutual assistance, collective responsibility, and modern secular education.

Among these builders who blazed the roads for future generations, there were no doubt a few individuals of Oriental origin, and even the first defense organization in Israel, "Hashomer," had been assisted by Yemenites and people from the Caucasus. However, these few only serve to accentuate the sad generality that the movement of Jewish revival had not aroused great repercussions among the Oriental Jewry in the country itself and abroad. (Z1:5)

The difference in the predisposition toward social change is an important factor in this phenomenon. An attempt to understand more fully these differences in motivation must lead to a comparison of the past social background of the two groups.

The social revolutions and the liberating movements in Europe had no doubt exerted a powerful influence on the trend of European Jewish public life. They aroused both the intellectual and the common man to greater interest in the conditions of the people. One cannot understand Zionism—the Auto-Emancipation movement of the Jewish people—without realizing that it was preceded by the European movements of Enlightenment and Humanitarianism.

On the other hand, the bulk of the Oriental Jewry had lived for centuries in Arab countries and was influenced by their social climate and pattern of life. A feudal land system, the exploitation of peasants and workers, the enslavement of women, a complete disregard of the rich for the poor, poverty, illiteracy, and technical backwardness are among the major characteristics of those countries.

The environment in which Oriental Jewry lived also patterned their conceptions and reactions. In the course of generations every one of these Jewish "tribes" had acquired a special mentality of its own. An illustration will make this point clearer.

The charge of "laziness" or "passivity" which is brought against Oriental Jews stems from a different sense of values. Many of the Orientals lack the drive of the Western Jews.

> Complaints are frequently voiced by administrators of immigrant camps that the Oriental Jews work only three days a week, instead of six; because in three days they earn enough for their very modest needs. Accustomed for generations to a spare diet and to primitive living conditions, they cannot suddenly and artificially increase their requirements— and they see no point in further labor. (S9:14)

Tahon (T6), comparing the two communities, says that the Ashkenazim belong to the middle class in their way of life, while the Orientals belong to the lower class. Even an Ashkenazi laborer has middle-class social and cultural needs. This is in large part due to the middle-class origin of many of these workers. (P5) Education and vocational preparation make social mobility easy and reduce class barriers.

But the Orientals lack these middle-class drives.

> It is a common phenomenon that big Oriental families live in one- or two-room apartments in slum areas, where the children must go to a most primitive school, in spite of having big savings in the bank. . . . A large percentage of Oriental laborers and artisans work only temporarily. The causes lie not only in the conditions of the labor market, and in illness, but to some degree in the instability of the Orientals' character. (T6:105)

The difference in motivation and drives between the two groups is most important for the understanding of their different values, outlooks, and patterns of behavior and, consequently, of their failure to integrate. An Oriental leader says:

There is a basic difference between us and our Ashkenazi brothers, and it is the dynamic energy which they have and we lack. It stems from the fact that they were persecuted much more than the Oriental Jewry. It made them creative, active, industrious and hard-driving people, who try to build a new world. Even when they pray, they cannot stand still. It is questionable if we have to be like them. It would be much better if they could be influenced by our Oriental calmness. But it is unquestionable that we have to become more like them, by becoming more dynamic. This dynamic energy is a power of creation, and it is the soul of Zionism. (Y4:3)

It is difficult to accept Yeshayahu's interpretation of the Ashkenazi dynamism. The cause of their dynamic energy lies not in their age-long persecution but rather in their education in the urban Western culture.

The "European personality" was molded through a long process of revolutions against and redemptions from economic and religious traditions which taught the individual to be submissive and resigned to his fate. Both capitalism and socialism stressed the importance of the individual and his power and right to determine his own future and reconstruct the world.

The Ashkenazi Jews belong to the Western middle class with its stress on achievement. Coming from the middle-class background, they are culturally motivated to suffer privations and to renounce immediate gratifications in order to achieve future goals.

The Oriental Jew who comes from the feudal Arab countries has never learned to believe in the power of the individual. In the social climate of the Arab countries, he did not have much of a chance to change and determine his own fate. The relative passivity and lack of drive of Oriental Jewry can only be explained against this cultural background.

In coming to Israel and meeting the Ashkenazi Jews, the Orientals, because of their lack of technical knowledge, their lack of readiness to change, and their relative passivity, were relegated to the position of the lower class. This only established their inferior status by depriving them of opportunities to change their pattern of motivation. A vicious circle was created which made the social integration of the two groups a more and more remote hope.

IV

Economic Differences

MOST ISRAELI WRITERS ON THIS TOPIC CONSIDER THE ECO-
nomic inferiority of the Oriental Jews the major problem in their adjustment. (T6, Y2) Although the economic factor should not be
underestimated, socio-psychological factors are also important in the
treatment of this problem.

A basic thesis of this study is that the central problem of the Oriental group is the crisis of discontinuity in their social and cultural life.
We witness a manifestation of a condition called "anomie"—the lack
of a well-organized system of values and norms which regulates the
behavior of the individual and sustains his mental health. It often
creates a marginal person of uncertain belongingness and a borderline
case of rootlessness. The application of Durkheim's concept of anomie
to the Oriental Jewry in Israel is elaborated by Eisenstadt in a 1948
pamphlet entitled *An Introduction to the Sociological Structure of
Oriental Jewry*. (E6) Some of the basic ideas to be presented here will
follow his lead.

The contact between the two Jewish groups resulted to a certain
degree in discontinuity in some aspects of the Oriental culture. Such
disruption is manifested in economic life, ethnic cohesiveness, customs,
family life, and education. The present chapter will deal with the economic aspects of this crisis; the following chapters will deal with the
other aspects.

This chapter will describe the lower economic status of the Orientals
in terms of occupations, standard of living, and so forth, and then will
elaborate the thesis that the difficulties of the Oriental Jews stem not

23

only from their poverty but also from the disruption in their previous economic structure.

Economic Differences and Their Impact

OCCUPATIONS

There is a marked difference between the two groups in technical skill and knowledge. The Oriental Jews came from countries which were backward in regard to technical development, while the Ashkenazim came to Palestine with the know-how of Western civilization.

The result is that "the Orientals have been relegated to the simpler and more primitive occupations, while the Ashkenazim are engaged in occupations calling for skilled knowledge. Thus the differences between the two groups have been further accentuated by an economic and social distinction." (Y2:13)

In the present economic order, built on unequal evaluation and remuneration of different jobs and vocations, this fact led to the rise of two distinct standards of living: a low one for the Orientals and a high one for the Ashkenazim.

Interpreting the results of a recent survey, Yeshayahu finds (Y3) that within the same vocational fields the Orientals have the unskilled tasks that are more difficult physically and less remunerative, while the Ashkenazim handle the skilled labor that is physically easier and more remunerative.

The Zionist emphasis on the normalization of the Jewish occupational structure led (around 1945) to establishment of "a small but healthy economic structure" (P5:63) based on agriculture and industry. This was true of the country's population as a whole, but not of the Oriental group.

> The status of these groups in the Israeli economy is similar to the status of the Jews, in the Diaspora, in the economy of the other nations— ecological concentration in cities, concentration in small trade and service, and the tendency to engage in vocations which are neglected, or even rejected, by the majority. (P5:66)

The low predisposition toward occupational change may be further illustrated by the tendency of each of the various Oriental groups to concentrate in a few branches of the economy. In other words, there is a clear occupational distinction not only between the Orientals and the Ashkenazim but also among the Oriental ethnic groups themselves. (P5)

This factor of "ethnic occupations" is a great barrier to the economic and social integration of the Israeli population. It strengthens the ethnic awareness, limits economic and social mobility, and perpetuates different ethnic standards of living. Sometimes it creates situations where one ethnic group is the employer, while the other is the employee.

The unhealthy occupational structure of the Orientals is a source of tension in the relationship between the two major groups, producing feelings of being discriminated against on the one hand, and attitudes of superiority on the other. As has already been stressed, the economic diffusion of the various Ashkenazi groups and immigrations was a major factor of their social integration. A policy of improving ethnic group relations must emphasize and work toward the productivization of the Orientals' occupational structure and their economic diffusion.

STANDARD OF LIVING, HOUSING, NEIGHBORHOODS

A study conducted in 1946 (C4) compared the standards of living of the two groups. Considering that the average Oriental family is much bigger than the Ashkenazi, the study shows that the average income per capita in 1946 was: Ashkenazim £.P. 8,002; Orientals £.P. 3,994. In other words: The average Ashkenazi could afford to spend exactly *twice* as much as an Oriental!

A comparison of the housing conditions according to communities throws into sharp relief the substantial differences between the two groups as far as congestion is concerned. The number of persons per room: Ashkenazim 2.70, Orientals 4.54. (C4)

Investigations which compare housing conditions of Oriental and Ashkenazi pupils in Jerusalem (B2) and Tel Aviv (E13) reveal similar results.

The Oriental ethnic groups tend to settle in compact neighborhoods with other immigrants from the same country, or even the same town. This gives them the feeling of being in familiar surroundings where they hear their own language and follow former customs. (P5, K7) Jerusalem, for instance, which until 1948 was the major center of Oriental Jewry, is divided into ethnic neighborhoods. In many cases, these sections are even called after the name of the ethnic groups.

Since 1911, there has been a Yemenite quarter near almost every one of the large villages. (P5) A study (B4) made in 1949 of the housing conditions in these Yemenite sections showed that families of four to seven, and sometimes even of eight to ten, were crowded into one-room apartments.

Being poor materially, and sometimes also lacking the initiative to improve their housing conditions, the Orientals allowed most of their neighborhoods to develop into slum areas. This only increased the barriers and social distance between the Orientals and the Ashkenazim, the latter making every effort not to live in these areas.

Today almost every Israeli city is divided into the "right side of the tracks" (the nice neighborhoods) and the "wrong side of the tracks." In the overwhelming majority of cases, this division coincides with the ethnic division into Ashkenazi and Oriental neighborhoods.

FAMILY SIZE

The Oriental family has a much higher birth rate than the Ashkenazi. (B1) The attitude of many Oriental families toward family planning is illustrated by the proverb of the prolific Yemenite women: "When there is no child in the belly, the belly is sad."

Investigating child mortality Bacchi says: "Taking the mortality of the Ashkenazim as 100, we find that the Sephardi figures are 152, and the other Orientals 263." (B1:126) The Israeli health services have sharply reduced the rate of infant mortality among the Orientals. For instance, the infant mortality rate of the Jews in Yemen was forty to fifty per cent, while among the Yemenite new immigrants it is only eight to ten per cent. (S9)

The high birth rate and lowered mortality rate, then, explain the existence of big Oriental families. One study (C4) showed that by the end of World War II the average size of an Oriental family was 6.4, while an Ashkenazi family consisted of only 4.3 persons. It need hardly be added that the big family is a factor that intensifies the housing and economic difficulties of the Oriental group.

HEALTH AND NUTRITION

Its low income and its large size make the Oriental family more susceptible to disease than the Ashkenazi family. On this question, Bacchi says:

Since Orientals are poorer than Ashkenazim, it is not clear whether community or economic status, or both, influence the incidence of the disease—the rates show that probably both factors operate in each income group. Ashkenazim have a lower incidence than Orientals; among the Ashkenazim the incidence decreases rapidly with income, while among the Orientals the decrease is less clear. (B1:123)

It is difficult to state how much the malnutrition of some Oriental sections may be attributed to their ethnic habits of nutrition. A study on "the influence of the community on the nutritional status of the family" (B1) shows that the Ashkenazim manage to consume a considerably higher quantity of animal protein, while they show a decidedly lower intake of the following nutrients: calories, phosphorus, iron, vitamin A, and thiamin. The consumption of the following foodstuffs is greater among the Ashkenazim: meat, fish, milk, cheese, and eggs. The Orientals consume more bread, fats, legumes, vegetables, and fruit. The investigators conclude that it is impossible to define clearly whose food habits are better, as mistakes are made on both sides.

In interpreting the results of this study, it should be kept in mind that it compared groups which were similar in all respects except for the community to which they belonged. But in reality many of the Orientals, being poorer, are characterized by malnutrition.

There are basic differences in the methods of food preparation, so that one may speak about two patterns of nutrition in Israel—the Ashkenazi and the Oriental. These differences are mentioned by Polack (P5) as a source of difficulty in adjustment, mainly for Oriental children who eat in cafeterias (in schools, camps, or collective settlements) which are run by Ashkenazim. Awareness of these differences may prevent tension in many situations, especially when the Ashkenazi group works with Oriental children.

SOCIAL WELFARE AND ASSISTANCE

Many of the impoverished Oriental families must apply for social welfare. A study on the "economic standard and receipt of public assistance" (B1:131) shows: (1) that at the same income level dependence is higher among the Orientals than among the Ashkenazim; (2) that dependence on the Jewish welfare organizations increases rapidly with the increasing size of the family, but at the same time is considerably higher for Orientals than for Ashkenazim; and (3) that as a result of the facts mentioned above, and because Oriental families are poorer and larger, their proportion among those assisted is by far larger than their proportion among the population.

There exists a large network of social welfare services throughout the country, agencies developed by the Jewish community during the mandate period when the British government did little to foster their development. Much of the work of these agencies is constructive, both preventive and curative; but part of it is also philanthropic, with all the demoralizing effects which accompany philanthropy.

The social welfare agency, in many instances, is a scene of most humiliating and degrading experiences and is a source of interpersonal conflicts and intergroup tensions, which breed low morale. A participant observer has recorded (in a social welfare agency) the following quite typical scene:

> In the corner of the room there is a big pile of clothes; in the middle sits a social worker and two gate keepers to see that no one takes clothes without permission. In the room a long line of immigrants, mainly Orientals and only few Ashkenazim, is waiting. The immigrants bargain with the social worker. When she sets a price almost everyone claims that the clothes are worthless and that others received better clothes. There are complaints and accusations of discrimination and Yiddish favoritism. Two Moroccans bang on the table and threaten that unless the social worker lowers the price, they will commit suicide or leave the country. Two Yemenite women plead and cry. The social worker lowers the price and gradually they come to an agreement. Leaving the room, one of the Moroccans tells his friends that he has outsmarted the social worker and that generally in this country one can get things only by shouting. (E6:116)

The dependency on the social welfare organizations is accompanied, in many cases, by strong feelings of ethnic jealousy, tension, and discrimination. For instance, a Moroccan immigrant says to a social worker: "In spite of the fact that they earn money, you support many Polish and Yiddish people; but when you see a Moroccan home that is clean, you don't want to give money." (E4:119)

These typical scenes are manifestations of the maladjustment and frustration of many people (mainly Orientals) who have lost the security of stable and positive group norms. They are symptoms showing that these social welfare recipients see themselves not as active participants and full-fledged members in the social life and institutions, but only as objects of philanthropy. Consequently they see the social organizations as a tool for exploitation and for the maximization of personal benefits.

This situation is symptomatic of a group of people, much larger than the group of recipients themselves, who see themselves—in relation to the social institutions—only as receivers and not as givers, only as people who are entitled to privileges but who do not have obligations.

Because of some negative aspects and effects of the social welfare organizations, there is a need for re-examination of their role and methods in the light of the broader issue of generating leadership, creating initiative and impetus in people to recreate their own lives and participate actively in the social life of the country. This last issue, as it is related to ethnic group problems, will be discussed in other chapters.

INTENSIFICATION OF CLASS DIFFERENCES

Post-1948 countrywide statistical surveys do not provide any classification of income, vocation, or housing according to ethnic groups. This may be part of a policy of de-emphasizing the ethnic differences, or of not hurting people's feelings by asking them for their ethnic origin.

It is reasonable to assume, however, that the class differences between the Orientals and the Ashkenazim have not been reduced but, on the contrary, have been increasing. The immigration of hundreds of thousands of impoverished, unskilled, and almost naked Orientals, accompanied by a general drop of the standard of living, intensified the class tensions and increased the class distance. Eisenstadt writes: "A large part of the new immigration entered special economic sectors—mainly public works. These jobs are temporary, do not demand much skill, are of low status and very unremunerative." (E4:31) While this statement also applies to the new Ashkenazi immigrants, it is especially true in regard to the Orientals, who are far less adaptable.

The fact that the majority of immigrants and especially Orientals were housed in deserted Arab villages and towns or new, cheap rooms and huts has only increased the social distance and intensified the socio-economic differences.

Culture Contact and Economy

The Oriental Jews in their origin-lands were accustomed to another form of economic organization. Most of them were peddlers and craftsmen who supplied the needs of an agrarian society. Personal contact with the customer characterized their work and limited its scope.

The economy of the Western group is based on capitalistic and impersonal principles in which the producer has no direct firsthand contact with the specific customer. Few people now labor to satisfy their own needs or the needs of persons within their acquaintance, for the product of their labor supplies an impersonal market.

The impersonal and specialized economy of the Ashkenazim was much stronger than the Orientals' economy, and the latter had to adjust themselves to the new ways of earning a living. Some of them never succeeded in making the needed adjustments; their life history in Israel has been a continuous transition from one job to another. Some Orientals living on the borders between the Jewish and Arab cities have tried to establish economic relationship with the Arabs. The tense relations between the Jews and the Arabs, however, make these economic positions very unstable and unremunerative. (E6)

In the transition from Oriental to the Western Economy, many of the Orientals had to give up their status of independent workers (peddlers or artisans) and became unskilled and dependent workers, or employees. Yeshayahu says:

> In Yemen every Jew was an independent master. He worked at home, starting and finishing whenever he wanted. During his work, he used to teach his sons a vocation and the Torah. He had time to pray, and to participate in community activities, with no one pushing him to complete the job quicker. But here in this country the Yemenites became employees who are pushed by foremen to work harder and faster. They lost their control of their own time, and together with it the warmth of the family circle. Dining outside the home, hunting for jobs in the evenings and hurrying to them in the mornings, left the family head without any time to teach the children Torah and enjoy family life. (Y5:47)

The Oriental is attracted by the material superiority of the Ashkenazi culture. The desire to acquire Western comforts, and especially modern clothes, puts pressure on the meager family budget. The low income of the Oriental (especially in comparison to his new higher economic needs) in many cases must be supplemented by the earnings of his wife and children (usually his daughters). Polack says:

> The low remuneration of women's work results in the fact that a woman's job is usually conceived merely as a transitional stage prior to her becoming a housewife. But Oriental women differ in this respect: because of the husband's low income, the woman has to work even after marriage. (P5:208)

Because of the women's lack of vocational preparation, jobs for Oriental women are limited in the overwhelming majority of cases to household services, especially floor scrubbing and laundry. The difference between the Oriental and Ashkenazi ways of cooking makes it difficult to employ the former as cooks.

The fact that many Oriental women must work outside the home, and especially the fact that they are taking care of other households, has had a detrimental effect on their own families. Yeshayahu says:

> In Yemen the father used to work and earn a living, while his wife reigned at home like a queen, and managed her household. His sons learned from his Torah and the vocation until they married and became independent artisans. His daughters lived at home, and waited for their marriage. While here in Israel, not only does the husband work hard, but his wife takes care of another woman's household, while her own home is cold and her children are neglected. The children also work for another employer. Consequently, the respect for and the status of the family head have deteriorated, and family cohesiveness has disintegrated. (Y5:47)

Summary

The difficulties of the Orientals stem not only from their poverty, but also from the discontinuity in their social and economic structure. This discontinuity is manifested in the transition from an autarchical to a specialized and impersonal economy, in which the Oriental has lost his status as an independent artisan, and has become an unskilled employee.

Another result of the cultural contact is the discontinuity of the family function as a guide in vocational and economic preparation, and a lowering of the status of the family head. Because of new economic needs, and low income, the Oriental women have to engage in unskilled jobs outside the home (in contrast to the customs in the lands of their origin), which results in undue stress in family relations.

Apart from the low economic status and the disruption of the previous economic structure of the Orientals, the difference in the socio-economic milieu between the Orientals and the Ashkenazim also serves as a source of frustration, feelings of being discriminated against, and— most important—self-depreciation. The aspiration for socio-economic mobility, almost unknown in the feudalistic society, makes the richer Ashkenazim become the reference group which the Orientals want to identify with and imitate. A difficult situation arises, wherein the Orientals share the common system of success symbols (accumulation of wealth) but are handicapped in the competition for such success by little formal education and few economic resources.

The growth of "status anxiety" and of emphasis on the value symbol of financial success (in contrast to the values of pioneering or national service) which characterizes the Israeli society in the last few years, and the widening economic gap between the old-timers (mainly Ashkenazim) and the new impoverished immigrants (mainly Orientals), are going to confront the nation with extremely grave problems of antisocial behavior and mental health. An application of Merton's analysis of "Social Structure and Anomie" to the Israeli scene points up some of the major factors contributing to this antisocial behavior problem:

> Poverty as such and consequent limitations of opportunity are not sufficient to induce a high rate of criminal behavior. . . . It is only when poverty, limited opportunity and a commonly shared system of success symbols are interrelated, that we can explain the higher association between poverty and crime in our society than in others where rigidified class structure is coupled with differential class symbols of achievement. (M5:681)

Ethnic sensitivity and awareness only aggravate the situation, serving as means of rationalization for not accepting, or even for violating, the norms and moral imperatives "imposed by the other group." (G3)

The feelings and aspirations—shared by the Orientals—of national identity and equality ("We are all Jews") and the desire of the Orientals to accept the Ashkenazi way and standard of living only intensify the realization that in actual life there is an unbridged gulf separating the Ashkenazim from the Orientals. This results, in the Orientals, in feelings of resentment, apathy, and self-depreciation, and sometimes in aggressive behavior.

V

Differences in Physical Appearance, Mannerisms, Clothing, and Language

DIFFERENCES BETWEEN THE ORIENTALS AND THE ASHKE-
nazim in Israel, in physical appearance, gestures, mannerisms, and
sometimes in clothing (especially among the older generation and newcomers), make ethnic awareness more pronounced.

Physical Appearance

The Jewish people in the Diaspora have in the course of centuries
split up into many different groups. Every country has left a distinctive
imprint upon the Jews domiciled in it. They have been influenced by
its culture and its language, and have even come to bear a facial resemblance to their Gentile fellow citizens. In fact, Jews in certain countries bear a closer resemblance to their non-Jewish compatriots than to
Jews in other countries.

While in most cases it is impossible to distinguish between the various Western groups on the basis of physical appearance, the difference
between the Orientals and the Ashkenazim is very distinctive.

Gestures and Mannerisms

A study of the gestural behavior of Italian and Jewish immigrants
in New York (E3) demonstrates that there are standardized group differences in the gestural behavior of certain ethnic groups, and that social
stimulation rather than so-called racial descent seems to have been the
determining factor for the assimilated (in contrast to the traditional)
Italians and Jews.

33

Subjective observation shows the same trend in Israel. An hypothesis that has to be investigated scientifically is that the small middle-class Oriental stratum tries to imitate the Ashkenazi pattern of gesture, mannerism, speech, etc. (a trend toward assimilation), while the lower Oriental and Ashkenazi classes influence each other (a trend toward mutual assimilation).

Clothing

The Ashkenazim have exercised a powerful influence upon the Orientals with regard to clothing. Patai says that in the beginning of the Ashkenazi immigration "it was but natural that the European Jews were influenced by the common Arab and Oriental Jewish style of dressing," (P2:19) but after a few years the Ashkenazi style became more prevalent.

> The old generation (grandparents) sticks to the traditional style of dressing; the intermediate generation (parents) adjusts gradually to the new style, but sometimes looks grotesque; while the younger generation tends to wear the modern clothes. (E6:26)

Of special importance for this study are the psychological problems (as in parent-child relations) involved in changing from one style of dress to the other. The Israeli literature does not deal with this issue. There is need for further study of this area, with emphasis on the psychological problems involved and the role of education in helping children and parents to solve them.

In this particular area, as in intergroup education in general, respect for cultural and ethnic differences must be the constant concern of the educator.

Language

Language is a factor which unites and also differentiates the two groups.

The Ashkenazim and the Orientals differ in their language background. The Yiddish language was for generations the Ashkenazim's mother tongue. It was the language of daily life and of literature, and a link that unified the various Ashkenazi subgroups throughout the Western world. In spite of the fact that Hebrew is now the official language in Israel, many Ashkenazim continue to speak Yiddish in the family circle, and to enrich their Hebrew with Yiddish expressions and anecdotes.

A classification of the Orientals on the basis of language background (S9:7) places them in three main language groups: (1) Arabic—a Semitic language spoken in Iraq, Syria, Yemen, Aden, Egypt, Libya, Tunisia, Algeria, and Morocco; (2) Ladino—a Hebrew-Spanish dialect used by Sephardim and in the Balkans; and (3) Persian—an Indo-European language spoken in Iran, Afghanistan, and Bakhara.

A study of the usage of the Hebrew language among the Oriental Jewry in Jerusalem in 1937 showed that Hebrew was seldom used *at home.* "Among the Yemenites and Sephardim, and to a lesser extent among the Moroccans, it is heard as a second language." (P5:32) The number of people who speak Hebrew has increased since then, except among the new immigrants.

The continued use of Yiddish by many Ashkenazim, concomitant with the use of the above-mentioned languages by many Orientals, perpetuates the differences and the distance between the two major groups.

THE HEBREW LANGUAGE

Two major factors are responsible for the revival of the Hebrew language: (1) the conviction of the Zionist leaders in Israel and abroad that the reconstructing of the Jewish culture and nation is impossible without a revival and modernization of the old Biblical language; and (2) the fact that the Israeli population is composed of many subgroups which have no common language background, and no one of them was ever in an overwhelming majority so to determine the language of the country. Hebrew was the only "neutral language" respected by all the ethnic groups, although unused in daily life by most of them. (P5)

Theodor Herzel, the creator of modern political Zionism, was, a mere fifty years ago, so skeptical about the fitness of Hebrew to serve as a colloquial medium as to say, "Who of us can ask for a railway ticket in Hebrew?" Today modern Hebrew is the language used by the majority of people in Israel. Being the only medium of education in the Jewish public schools, it has become the natural mother tongue for the overwhelming majority of the new Israeli-born generation.

As such it has been the medium of new cultural values, usages, and traditions: "folk songs, folk dances, a modern literature, the theatre and so on, filled the void which inevitably followed the abandonment of the old traditions." (E8:164)

The Hebrew language thus became a most dynamic unifier of the various ethnic groups. But it is at the same time a medium of ethnic differentiation. In spite of the fact that the overwhelming majority of the Israeli-born generation speak Hebrew, their accents differ according to community origin: Israeli-born Ashkenazim, and Israeli-born Orientals. (The last group is divided mainly into two, one having a Yemenite, and the other a Sephardic, accent.)

The difference between the origin languages of the two tribes, the differences in accent in pronouncing the Hebrew language, and the usage of their respective foreign languages by new immigrants, make the two groups aware of their ethnic origin.

THE PROBLEM OF LANGUAGE TRANSFORMATION

Education is confronted with the problem of creating a common language background for the whole nation. The importance of the Hebrew language as a unifier of ethnic groups and as a means of cultural and social integration cannot be overemphasized. The crucial question, however, is how to bring about this language transformation without creating stress, emotional difficulties, and anomie. This point needs elaboration.

On coming to Israel the modern Ashkenazi group has abandoned the Yiddish language almost entirely and begun to speak Hebrew. Being imbued with aspirations to reconstruct the Jewish culture, they did not find it difficult (psychologically speaking) to acquire and develop the new language. The feeling of participation in the creation of a new language only bolstered the morale of the Ashkenazi group, and gave it a sense of worthiness, status, and fulfillment in a historic mission. The feeling of being (after two thousand years) the first Jewish generation to speak Hebrew was a source of pride and security.

This social outlook and emphasis on change led also to some negative results. A chauvinistic atmosphere was created, in which the usage of "foreign" languages (especially outside the home) was seen as unpatriotic. The Yiddish language became the main target of attack: people who continued to speak Yiddish were called "old-fashioned, ridiculous, and ghettoish." Public opinion banned the publication of Yiddish newspapers and literature.

These chauvinistic attitudes led to a widening of the gap between the modern Ashkenazi group and the small "old population community" which objected to Hebrew and continued to use Yiddish. With regard to the Oriental groups, the emphasis on "Hebrew only" naturally excluded any attempt at social and cultural activities in the mother tongue of those communities.

As has already been stressed, the Oriental groups are not characterized by predisposition toward change and a vision of cultural reconstruction. Being anxious and insecure (like every immigrant group in the world), they cling to the old symbols of security, one of which is the mother tongue. They have been relatively slow in adapting to the new medium of communication—the Hebrew language.

The stress on "Hebrew only" (especially in public activities) and the attitude of looking down on "exile-languages," became a factor which contributed toward the disorganization of the ethnic groups' communal life and to the disintegration of the groups themselves. Conditions characterized by cultural anomie were created. On the one hand, many of the Oriental people did not identify fully with the new language as a medium of expression and creativity; on the other hand, the traditional languages were looked down on as inappropriate for social and cultural activities. The result was a cultural vacuum which was dangerous to the mental health of the group and the individual.

The language transformation problem is an undisguised source of conflict and antagonism between many Oriental parents and their children. It exemplifies the fundamental difference between the orientation of the parents who cling to the symbols of the past, and the orientation of the children who look toward modern modes of behavior (in this case the Hebrew language).

While the stress on speaking only Hebrew became a constructive force in the life of the Ashkenazi group by "filling the void which inevitably followed the abandonment of the old traditions," (E8:164) it had some detrimental effects on the life of the other less dynamic and adaptable groups. The dominant Ashkenazi group is too ethnocentric in thinking that what is good for them is also good for other groups.

Under the impact of the recent huge immigration, the taboo against using "exile" languages in public life (lectures or entertainment) has been relaxed. At present many foreign language newspapers are published in the land. In 1949 a research institute (I2) studied the public's opinion on the question: Do the foreign language newspapers accelerate or impede the cultural absorption of the new immigrants? The results, tabulated according to the percentages of the various population elements that were in favor of or against such newspapers, were as follows:

	Against	For
Israeli population	57%	43%
Israeli born	70%	30%
New immigrants	59%	41%

In spite of the fact that there is an enormous shift in the direction of accepting the inevitability of the use of foreign languages, the majority of the public sees them as a threat to the Israeli culture.

A policy of improving ethnic group relations should operate on the following principles, in dealing with the language problem:

1. Encourage the learning and use of the Hebrew language, not only through schooling, but also through informal association of Hebrew-speaking and non-Hebrew-speaking Israelis.

2. Respect and accept the various ethnic accents in pronouncing Hebrew. Close social relationships between groups will lead to a gradual elimination of ethnic accents.

3. Avoid putting any social stigma on the use of "exile languages."

4. Encourage communal activities led in foreign languages and gradually enlarge the role of Hebrew in these activities.

5. Accept the foreign language papers, and gradually increase the part of Hebrew in them.

6. Appreciate the contribution of foreign languages toward cultural enrichment.

7. Help immigrants' children (who are quicker than their parents in learning Hebrew) to appreciate the emotional role the foreign mother tongue plays in their parents' lives.

8. See the whole question of language transformation as related to the emotional, social, and economic security of the ethnic groups. The person who feels accepted is much more ready to change than is the person who does not.

VI

Disintegration of the Communal Life
of the Orientals

THE CONTACT BETWEEN THE ASHKENAZIM AND THE ORIEN-
tals resulted in a crisis in the continuity and the cohesiveness of the
Orientals' way of life. This in turn adversely affected the mental health
of the Orientals as individuals and as a group.

An examination of the social structure and organization of the
Oriental groups may further illustrate and substantiate this point.

On coming to Israel, the Oriental groups were (and to a certain degree are still today) organized into groups—called *Landsmanschaften*—
differentiated according to country of origin. (P5:12) The major organizations are those of the Sephardim and the Yemenites. The task of
these institutions is to support and direct the lives of their members and
to organize them into ethnic entities.

Eisenstadt lists the following major characteristics of these cohesive
ethnic groups:

1) Extensive stable relations between clusters of families, neighbors,
etc. 2) Maintenance of communal religious centers. 3) Existence of the
old traditional elites and continuity of relations between the elites and
the various families of this group through guidance of communal affairs
and supervision of the individual's personal life. 4) Continuity of a relatively strong informal communal public opinion and social control. 5)
Some degree of formal communal organization—*Landsmanschaften*,
specific ethnic local groups, etc.—established on a personal and patriarchal basis. (E4)

Despite individual differences the people in these groups are in
major agreement as to the meaning of life and the rights and responsibilities of the individual.

39

The modern Ashkenazi group, except for one small Orthodox group, (P5:15) almost never organized its institutions on an ethnic basis. They established voluntary and democratic institutions based on political parties, with the hope that all the Jews in Palestine, regardless of ethnic origin, would participate in and benefit from them. These powerful organizations took over the various political, social, and economic functions, and made the role of the Oriental ethnic institutions seem very secondary and sometimes even unpatriotic.

A gradual diminution of the ethnic group control and a deterioration of the ethnic organizations among the Orientals have already started. Underlying this process is the aspiration of the Orientals, mainly of the young generation, to imitate and integrate with the Ashkenazi culture, with its greater freedom and economic security.

The attempts of various Oriental leaders to participate in non-ethnic general institutions as delegates of their ethnic groups have not been very successful. Thus, until the First World War, the Sephardim were the dominant section among the Palestinian population. (P2) Now they find themselves subject to the influence of the new majority. At one time they were the cultural and intellectual elite of Palestinian Jewry; now they have been ousted from this position, too, by the Ashkenazim. For these reasons they are trying to unite the Oriental Jews around them—but with very little success. The various Oriental groups, especially the Yemenites, are unwilling to recognize the Sephardi hegemony. (Y2) Even many of the Sephardim themselves do not support, and do not identify themselves with, their "ethnic committees."

Individuation and Secularization

The disorganization of the communal life of the Orientals may be understood as one of the phenomena associated with immigration.

Immigration has characteristic effects on the behavior of people. It causes disorganization of some of the most important and essential channels of cooperation. One of the requirements for healthy development of the individual is full membership in a cohesive community. "The migrant is separated from such membership and therefore becomes increasingly *individuated* as the length of separation increases." (F1:738)

The individuation process is manifested in the loosening of the ties between the family and the communal organization.

The immigrants always undergo a process of diminution and shrinkage of their fields of social participation. This is due mainly to the state of social and psychological insecurity in which they live. (E5:8)

To illustrate, an Oriental immigrant says that, in Israel, "he does not like to meet his Moroccan friends, because he is ashamed to meet them; there they were real men, but here they are worthless stones." (E4:12)

These feelings of insecurity, confusion, and disappointment are strengthened by the fact that the individual lacks the moral and emotional support of his communal group which is so important in a period of stress.

The professed national aspiration of social and cultural integration and elimination of all ethnic barriers was another factor which contributed toward the disintegration of communal feeling and belongingness of the Orientals.

An atmosphere in which ethnic differences and loyalties were ignored and considered taboo or unpatriotic was created. The blueprint was: ethnic symbols of identification have to be destroyed for the sake of social integration. This meant (to translate this fantastic blueprint into the language of reality) building new organizational structures, instead of rebuilding and modernizing the old ones. The modern institutions led by the Ashkenazim ignored the traditional organizations of the Orientals—religious centers, and ethnic local or countrywide committees. Consequently these Oriental institutions lost much of their power and influence.

The new social forms of modern Palestine have had sufficient dynamic power to shatter the old Oriental tradition and value system. They did not succeed, however, in reconstructing a new cohesive form of life. Social consensus, one of the primary sources of personal stability, has deteriorated to the point of a breakdown in primary group relations, and the individual has become more or less isolated.

A field of anomie has been created—a lack of cohesive group norms. Applying Erich Fromm's analysis of the positive and negative meaning of freedom to the Oriental's culture in Israel, one can say that the Oriental

. . . has been freed from traditional authorities, and has become an Individual; but at the same time he has become isolated, powerless, and an instrument of purposes outside of himself, alienated from himself and others; furthermore, this state undermines his self, weakens and frightens him . . . (F11:270)

Immigration also has a secularizing effect.

The resident of a stable community who knows of no other way of life, takes for granted the customs of his community. But the migrant observes people living quite naturally under different systems. The usual effect of exposure to a different culture is secularization of attitudes and beliefs. (F1:738)

The most important single function of a cohesive community is the exercise of informal social control. The conduct of the individual is regulated by the public opinion of the group he belongs to, which serves as a basis for morality and adjusted behavior. No amount of legislation, no police force or any other law-enforcing agency, can substitute for the role of the public opinion of the community in promoting moral behavior.

Under the impact of the cultural contact with the Ashkenazi way of life, the Orientals' group norms were weakened, and community life was secularized and deteriorated.

An example of the secularization effect is seen in the field of religion. While in some other countries the religious centers try to broaden their activities and become community centers, in Israel the synagogue has remained mainly a place of prayer. Once the center of community life, it is losing its unifying power, especially for the young generation. Frankenstein says:

> The religious values of Judaism lack content and meaning for the majority of the Oriental youth. Many of the Oriental parents remain rooted in tradition, but their educational weakness and inability to understand the new social reality and demands result in resistance and protest on the part of the young generation and in the abandonment of the tradition. This process is accelerated by the fact that, in many cases, even the parents' orthodoxy has become a meaningless formality of no directive power in everyday life. (F7:146)

This trend toward secularization is very strong and has its impact even on the youth among the new Oriental immigrants. In a recent study of the acculturation of young Yemenite immigrants, Rieger found that

> among many of these youths, a process of secularization has begun: cutting of the earlocks, unobservance of the rituals, and so forth; these are signs of the replacement of the religious value system by a national and secular spirit. . . . Most conflicts with the parents are concerned with religious matters. (R4:262)

The diminishing importance of religion in the communal and family life underlie the disintegrative processes working in the Oriental groups and the tension prevailing in their family life. The crucial point, however, is not the disintegration process per se, but rather the fact that it was not accompanied by an acceptance of a constructive and positive system of values. (In significant contrast is the acceptance by the Ashkenazi group of the dynamic Zionist ideology.)

The Oriental Leadership

Another major characteristic of the crisis in the Oriental culture is the disintegration of the role of the traditional leaders. The role of leaders in Oriental cultures is more crucial than in the Western one, because fewer issues are left to the free choice and decision of the individual.

The importance of the leaders in an era of stress cannot be overemphasized. "They interpret and communicate the ultimate social values and serve as symbols of security and identification with the social system." (E7:222) An Oriental immigrant explains the importance of the traditional leaders in the following words:

> It is entirely different here from the way things were in Morocco; we did not encounter such problems there. Everything was more or less settled there, and whenever any difficulty arose, we had some people like A. who knew what it meant. It is very good that they [the leaders] are here also. When they explain all these things, they do not seem so strange and terrible. (E7:227)

The traditional Oriental leaders, confronted with a new way of life and new requirements, find it difficult to live up to their role of interpreting the new social values and of serving as symbols of security. The dominant Western culture of Israel, the complicated bureaucratic structure of the State, the competitiveness of the political parties—all these become confusing and bewildering problems.

From the point of view of social integration and mutual assimilation, the loosening of the ties between the leaders and the ethnic community is a negative process. It has been shown that "the extent of social participation of the immigrants with the new country is functionally related to the extent of relations existing between the immigrants and the members of the elites." (E7:223)

A social policy which supports only the traditional elites and which endows them with ruling power may stop the growth of the ethnic communities and create tension between the progressive and conservative sectors. Such a method recalls the attempts of the British government to perpetuate the original and conservative features of some African tribes by supporting the reactionary "old guard" leadership. This policy of so-called indirect rule is based on the false assumption that the traditional ethnic institutions continue to represent the aspiration and value system of these tribes despite their contact wih Western culture.

Copying this British policy would mean a deliberate attempt to freeze the development of the Oriental people and to check their progressive and adaptable capacities. It would result in the revolt of the liberal elements rather than a relatively peaceful and evolutionary development.

A social policy of re-educating the traditional elites and mainly of encouraging younger and more modern leaders to achieve strategic positions in their communities would have led to a constructive growth in the value system of the Orientals, and would have prevented the creation of the anomie conditions. Even now, such a policy might lead to strengthening of the Orientals' predisposition toward change, to a cultural synthesis based on the values of the two cultures, and consequently to a neutralization of ethnic belongingness—in short, to social integration.

Many of the Orientals themselves are looking to a new type of leadership which will symbolize the synthesis of the Oriental and the Ashkenazi way of life. Studying Yemenite immigrant youth, Rieger (R4) found that there is on the one hand a decline in the prestige of the traditional leaders ("the scholars"), due to their inability to adjust to new conditions, and on the other hand a rise of a younger leadership. The leader among the youth is the boy who manages to integrate the new and the traditional patterns of behavior, yet does not wholly reject his ethnic customs.

The ultimate professed aim of both Israeli ethnic groups is the emergence of homogeneous national entities which would positively synthesize the values contributed by the different peoples. The main reason for this ideal stems from the specific Jewish background and character of all the groups, and the mutual Jewish identification which exists between the immigrants and the old-timers, or between the Ashkenazim and the Orientals. Nevertheless, this national aspiration of social integration could be promoted only by the rise of a new dynamic and "synthetic" Oriental leadership.

The social policy (or lack of it) which led to the deterioration of the Orientals' formal communal organizations was based on the assumption that they would grow *individually* into sharing and participating in the modern form of life. This assumption proved unfounded. (E7) The nature of the cultural contact between the two groups led to the dissolution of the previous pattern of relationships between the Oriental groups and their leaders, to the weakening of the feelings of belongingness in Oriental communities, and to isolation and individuation of the Orientals. It did not lead, however, to a mass movement of participation, on behalf of the Oriental people, in the new forms of life and institutions: "The movement of Jewish revival had not aroused great repercussions among the Oriental Jewry." (Z1:5)

Lewin (L4) proved experimentally that the best way to bring about a change in the behavior of the individual is through a process of *changing the norms of his group*. The group supports and encourages the individual in his new way. On the one hand, the group creates new norms to identify with, and on the other hand it helps to avoid the conflict of marginality and double loyalty.

A recent study of the role of elite and primary groups in the absorption of new immigrants substantiates the validity of Lewin's theory:

> It has been amply demonstrated in almost all of our cases that any kind of integration into the new social system could be effected only by changing the roles, values and social perceptions of these groups *and not by breaking them up* or neglecting them. (E7:223)

The difficulties of a non-cohesive ethnic group are illustrated in another study of the adaptation of new immigrants in Israel. (G3) This study shows that a group which was not secure in its Jewish belongingness and identification in the Diaspora (a group like the Moroccan Jewry, for instance) will find it more difficult to adjust to the new land than a cohesive Jewish group such as the Yemenites. Contact with the French culture resulted in the disintegration of the Jewish community in Morocco, and created ambivalent feelings toward Judaism. The process of disintegration of the Moroccan community continues in Israel. It is manifested in disintegration of the family life (E6, T7), in the very high rate of juvenile delinquency (F7:148), and in some cases in non-identification with, and a negative attitude toward, the Israeli social structure (G3:175).

There is a danger that the contact between the Ashkenazi and Oriental cultures will lead to similar results. There is already much evidence that the process leading to anomie has started even among some formerly cohesive groups of Oriental Jewry. For instance, Frankenstein found that "in general the symptoms of waywardness among Oriental youth in Tel Aviv are much more severe than among the Oriental youth in Jerusalem." (F7:149) There is much less culture contact between the Orientals and the Ashkenazim in Jerusalem than in Tel Aviv; consequently the Oriental communities in Jerusalem are much less individuated and secularized, and tend more to continue in a cohesive pattern of living. This illustration shows again the detrimental effects of a non-cohesive community.

A basic hypothesis of this paper is that one way to mutual assimilation is through a gradual transformation of the feelings of ethnic identification and of the social perceptions of the Orientals. This can be done only by a process of changing the norms of the ethnic groups, and not by breaking them up. This study is based on a frame of reference which may seem paradoxical: the way to mutual assimilation is through activating and strengthening the social life of the Oriental ethnic communities. The Oriental leaders are thus thrust into key positions of being potential agents of social change! (E7)

In discussing the social welfare and assistance problem, it was pointed out that some of the social welfare recipients are representative of a much bigger group of people who see themselves, in relation to the social institutions, merely as receivers, but not as givers; only as people entitled to privileges, but sharing no obligations. The majority of these people come from the Oriental groups.

The failure to support and encourage the rise of a constructive Oriental leadership largely explains the lack of initiative, active social participation, and civic awareness in these communities. And to a great extent, the dominant Ashkenazi group is responsible for this situation.

In the past, endeavors to help the Orientals took three major directions: economic assistance, vocational preparation, and education of children. (E6) We do not deny the importance of these activities, nor do we doubt the devotion of the Ashkenazim who tried to help the Oriental community. We shall attempt, however, to point out some mistakes in the way these activities (many of them philanthropic projects) have been administered. They have not devoted enough attention to the need for generating leadership and creative impetus among the Orientals.

The problem is not only the financial and administrative one of providing technical facilities, machines, housing, and schools; the main problem is helping the Orientals to use the facilities and exploit the opportunities. In short, the major problem is to help the Orientals to help themselves!

The basic mistake of the Ashkenazi group lies in their failure to encourage creative leadership in the Orientals. Says an Oriental writer:

> It cannot be denied that whether by accident or by design, the rapidity of immigration from Europe has led to a certain neglect of the potentialities of the Sephardim, in common with those of all the Oriental communities. The European Jews know themselves better, they prefer their own people and place greater reliance in their own leaders, with the result that the Sephardim have to some extent been pushed aside. (Y2:5)

There is no research evidence to prove the validity of this claim. It is a known fact, however, that the Sephardi group (which has many potentialities for leadership, since it occupies the highest economic and educational level among all the Oriental communities) feels rejected, pushed aside, and discriminated against by the Ashkenazi leadership.

Being always on the "receiving end" and having to depend on the Ashkenazi community has demoralizing effects on the Orientals. These ill effects are manifested mainly in: (1) feelings of inadequacy and resentment, (2) a dependent pattern of behavior, (3) misconceptions of some social norms, and (4) misconception of the role of leadership. These points need some more elaboration.

These statements of a Yemenite leader testify to the feelings of resentment created in the Oriental group by the condition of economic dependency.

> The equality of rights is given to us by the Ashkenazim; they have the power and they are the givers. Every donor who gives charity has some feelings of superiority. It is not easy or pleasant to be a recipient who is dependent on charity. Dependency is not a healthy framework for relations of equality and friendship. Relieve us from our dependency on you! (Y4:3)

> The Yemenites feel that the ruling group (the Ashkenazim) are doing everything only for their own benefit. The Yemenites strive to get rid of

the status of receivers and to become also rulers. It is the nature of a ruling group to underestimate the abilities and potentialities of the subordinate group. Consequently they are reluctant to entrust the Yemenites with responsible positions and cooperate with them on an equal basis. (Y1:12)

The laudable efforts of the Ashkenazi community to help the Orientals raise their standard of living have nevertheless proved largely abortive, mainly because of the failure to encourage the rise of a creative Oriental leadership. Instead of the semi-philanthropic approach to the Oriental problem, there is need for a program of mutual activity, based on cooperative planning and administration of projects by the Ashkenazim and Orientals together.

Another detrimental effect of these unfortunate conditions is that they tended to build other dependent relations between the Oriental and the Ashkenazi community, instead of either independent or interdependent relations. Instead of the Oriental groups gaining power to go ahead "under their own steam," they have tended to be less and less able to cope with their problems without the assistance of the Ashkenazi group.

An extreme illustration of an Israeli public policy which, despite its underlying good intentions to help and guide, unfortunately had detrimental effects of passivity and dependency is the establishment of special immigrant camps. Harman says:

> It was unfortunately necessary to establish immigrants' camps providing shelter and food. It was found, however, that some of the newcomers had lost the initiative and the impetus to recreate their own lives, viewed their future lethargically and were not inclined to move. (H2:307)

The insecure immigrants were rushed into camps wherein they lost their individuality by becoming mere numbers, all the movements of which were regulated by a formal and impersonal bureaucratic organization. The ethnic strangeness of the officials intensified the despair of the Oriental immigrant and his inability to make plans for the future. These frustrations resulted in a regression to immature behavior, characterized by social and emotional dependency on the officials, passivity, and impulsive behavior. (G3, E5)

The lack of initiative and the dependency of some Oriental communities is sometimes intensified by a different conception of the social norms of rights and obligations. By way of illustration, an Israeli magazine reports:

A small community of new Yemenite immigrants refused to leave their tents and move to the new houses, built especially for them by the Jewish Agency, and demanded to be transferred to the city. When it was explained to them that in the new place they would have to dwell in tents again they answered: We shall demonstrate once or twice and the Jewish Agency will give us houses. (S7)

This small community misinterpreted the role of the various organizations and their attempt to assist, and saw dependency on the Jewish Agency as the right and main way to solve their economic problems.

An agricultural consultant who instructs a new Oriental cooperative settlement reports his observations:

The settlers do not have a responsible attitude toward the property of the community. The attitude towards the equipment is as if it had been given to them as a gift. Their feeling is that any time they ask new equipment will be given again and again. (F10:46)

These examples illustrate the lack of drive of some of the new Oriental communities and their misinterpretation of the nature of the assistance given to them. They visualize the social institutions as paternalistic authorities that have to support their dependent sons.

There is an urgent need to support the rise of a modern Oriental leadership which will activate the social life of these communities and lead them toward using and benefiting from the facilities afforded to them, and toward enriching and extending these facilities. There is a danger, however, that these leaders will misuse their rights and will lead their communities in the easy road of dependency on the Ashkenazi group. Criticizing his own community, Yeshayahu says:

The Yemenites have many leaders whose main job is to demand help from others (the Ashkenazim). We would have achieved much more had we created funds and organizations for mutual help. Our leadership is not creative, but one which leads the community in the easy direction of begging, demanding and depending on others. (Y5:53)

The hyperactive political atmosphere and the extreme competitiveness among the various political parties only encourage (sometimes unwittingly) the creation of this type of leadership. Says Yeshayahu:

The political polarization results in a lot of bargaining for the support and votes of the Yemenites, who sometimes laugh at the stupidity of the competitors and take advantage of the circumstances by receiving help from both parties and laughing twice. (Y1:12)

Studies show that in some cases new Oriental immigrants and their leaders "belong" to a political party not because of any ideological identification, but because of economic calculations of benefit. (E4:157) The political party could be an educational power which unites the various groups through an atmosphere of ideological identification, and become a springboard for the elimination of social distance and tension between the Ashkenazim and Orientals. The political party could penetrate through the wall of ethnic grouping and establish ideological camps composed of various ethnic origins. The political party could become a meeting place for informal gathering of various ethnic groups (in contrast to the formal and bureaucratic relations which exist today). It could become a school for educating Oriental leaders who would go back to their own communities and organize its social life.

In actuality, however, the present political parties in Israel sometimes become, because of unscrupulous activity, a destructive and demoralizing force, helping into power an Oriental leadership that considers its main job to be the selling of the votes of its group to the highest bidder. Of course, this type of "bargaining leadership" does not achieve any of the positive objectives mentioned above. On the contrary, it creates in the Oriental people an attitude of cynicism toward the "hypocritical" political parties and the value system they claim to represent.

Summary

The cultural contact between Orientals and Ashkenazim has resulted in a crisis in the continuity of the Orientals' social structure, communal belongingness, value system, and relations to leadership. The various Oriental groups differ in the intensity of such disintegration, but all of them are affected by it. The traditional cohesive pattern of living was not replaced by acceptance of, and identification with, a new and positive scale of social values. This resulted in the creation of a dangerous field of anomie conditions which exemplify Fromm's interpretation of the concept of negative freedom. They constitute a source of feelings of futility, anxiety, and resentment in the life of the Oriental and his group.

A policy which aims at social integration and mutual assimilation must work toward activating the social life of the Oriental communities.

Conditions conducive to mutual assimilation will lead toward identification with the new social structure through a process of interaction and mutual modification.

The Oriental leaders are the potential social agents who are of greatest importance in this endeavor of bringing about a synthesis of the two cultures and social integration of the two ethnic groups. In many cases the Oriental leadership and its potentialities have been overlooked by the Ashkenazi community in its attempts to help the Orientals. This created, in the Oriental communities, feelings of resentment and a pattern of passive and dependent behavior, sometimes intensified by misconception of the role of the authorities. Unscrupulous activities of the political parties are a detrimental influence, tempting the Oriental community to exploit the circumstances. It jeopardizes the growth of a creative and dynamic Oriental leadership and hampers identification with the new social structure.

Part Three

THE ORIENTAL YOUTH

VII

Oriental Youth and the Family

A 1952 ARTICLE IN *The Jewish Frontier* ENDS ON THE FOL-
lowing hopeful note:

> There is an unqualified delight with which the entire population views
> and cherishes the numerous children of the Oriental communities. This
> is the best evidence of the country's faith in the One People that will
> emerge in a course of a generation. All temporary gaps in adjustment
> are bridged by the confident declaration—the children are wonderful.
> (S9:34)

The analysis undertaken in the present study leads to opposite conclusions. The present stage of anomie has detrimental effects, especially on the mental health of the Oriental youth. In many cases, it
creates a disintegrated and marginal person of uncertain belongingness.
The stage of marginality and rootlessness can lead to maladjustment and
antisocial behavior. If the present trend of anomie continues there is
danger that the hope of becoming "One people and a fruitful Jewry enriched by the traditions of the East and the dynamic energy of the
West," (S9:34) will become a more and more remote and unattainable
dream. In other words, there is danger that the adjustment of the
second-generation Orientals will be not smoother, but—on the contrary
—even more difficult, than that of their parents.

This realistic outlook is consistent with the analysis in the previous
chapter, which showed the detrimental effects of the cultural contact
between the Ashkenazim and the Orientals. This chapter will attempt to
further elaborate the same hypothesis and show that the contact between the two cultures is a source of strain and sometimes even disinte-

gration in the life of the Oriental family, and that this tension in the family has detrimental effects on the personality of the Oriental young people.

Tensions in the Oriental Family

The Oriental family in the origin lands had been of the patriarchal type, characterized by complete subordination of the wife and the children. The father's status as the head of the family was reinforced by the fact that in many cases he managed it as a producing and training unit. For instance, "In Yemen every Jew was an independent master, and during his work he used to teach his sons vocation and Torah." (Y5:47)

In Israel, gradual initiation of the children into the productive functions of the family (accompanied by subordination to the father, who is the foreman) hardly occurs at all. The reasons are mainly two: (1) The majority of the Orientals lost their status as independent workers and became employees. (2) Most of the children do not want to work at their fathers' occupations. Consequently, the Oriental family (and especially the father) has lost its role as a guide in vocational and economic preparation. (E6)

At present almost all Oriental youth over fourteen years of age are working and earning money. Sometimes they even support their families. Of course, these conditions of relative economic independence make them resent the fathers' attempts at subordinating them.

Because of the low income and new economic needs, many of the Oriental women have to engage in a job outside the home. Through firsthand experience they come to learn the Ashkenazi way of living and are impressed by the freedom of the Ashkenazi women. They become aware that there is a different and more desirable pattern of husband-wife relations. The attempts of the Oriental women to gain higher status in their families lead to conflicts with their husbands. (S3)

This brief discussion has already shown that the two basic relational components within the family structure (husband-wife and parent-child) are undergoing a radical change. The most crucial of the two is the crisis in parent-child relations. Warner and Srole, in a study of American ethnic groups, point out that

> The fundamental fact facing the ethnic parent is that, through changes forced upon the family structure . . . he has lost many of the indirect

controls *(economic, educative, recreational)* by which he had formerly maintained his all-inclusive authority over his children's behavior. (W2:127)

Observing and studying the problems of the Oriental parents in Israel, one comes to similar conclusions. As stressed above, many families lost their function as guides in economic and vocational preparation. Gradually the Oriental family also loses its educative function. The difficulties of adjustment which confront the Oriental immigrant consume the bulk of his physical, mental, and emotional energy. The pressure of adjustment leaves little room for working toward a cohesive frame of family unity and intimacy. The child who grows up in a family that is yielding under economic pressure and shattered by its efforts to find a place in society is unable to turn to his parents for guidance and support.

The conflicting attitude of the marginal child toward his family value system intensifies his difficulties in identifying with it and incorporating into himself the values, social standards, affection, and warmth which a family offers. The process of socialization, which develops through identification with parents and introjection of their interpretation of social behavior, must suffer severely under these unfortunate circumstances. Discussing parent-child relationships among many Oriental immigrants, Orny says:

> The parents are much more confused and bewildered than their children. The mother lags in her adaptation to the new conditions. Centering her existence around the home, she has no relations beyond it except with a few people of her own ethnic background. Instead of helping and guiding the child, she has to be guided by him. His importance increases and he feels that he no longer needs the guidance of his old-fashioned parents. (O5:4)

And Frankenstein, describing extreme cases of disintegrated Oriental families, says:

> The parents, especially the mothers, feel lost and bewildered. They do not understand at all the children's problems. They try to inject in their children feelings of resentment toward the new reality. Such attempts to tear the ties between their children and the new social structure only result in tearing the ties between their children and themselves. (F7:80)

The organization of leisure hours for recreation and for religious education and celebrations was centered, for the Oriental family, in the home. The holidays played an important educational role. These celebrations strengthened the relationship between the small family and the "extended family." But the secularization and individuating effects of the immigration, and the parent-child tensions, have made the Sabbath and the holidays an unimportant affair. "In some cases the children do not join their parents but spend the holiday in their own circle." (E6:27)

The Oriental family is based not only on patriarchal relations, but also on identification with the cultural traditions of the past. "In their leisure time, the parents enjoy non-Hebrew songs, stories, plays, etc." (O5:4) From the parents' point of view, any modification in traditional customs is a threat to family continuity and existence. Naturally, any attempt on the part of the children to open a new doorway to life is met with parental resistance. Speaking of similar ethnic problems in Yankee City, Warner and Srole say: "Parent and child are each eager to convert the other. Neither is amenable and hence, on specific issues clash is inevitable." (W2:144) The same can be said of the parent-child relationship among the Orientals.

Very little research has been done on the problems of the Oriental family. Most of such studies as have been made were made by social workers (T1, C4) or educators who work with wayward youth. (F7, S3) These studies deal mainly with the most disintegrated and maladjusted segment of the Oriental Jewry. The description of the family life of this segment is rather gloomy: a patriarchal and autocratic structure in which the father rules the family by using the rod. He is disinterested in the welfare of the family, and spends a large part of his income without considering the family needs. (E6) The family budget is unbalanced and most of the money is spent on food without any allotment for clothing or better housing. The father's attitude is one of indifference punctuated by spells of extreme aggression. (S3) The mother is submissive and emotionally depressed. (F7) In most cases she is illiterate. Her knowledge of hygiene and child care is very limited and often she handles her children according to superstitious practices. (S3) These superstitions are passed on to the children who begin to believe that ghosts and spirits direct and rule the world. (S1)

This gloomy picture does not represent the life pattern of the "average" Oriental family, but it shows in an extreme way the kinds of problems and tensions that often trouble such a family.

The Problem of Marginality

The Oriental youth resembles the minority group members in America, in their oscillation and uncertainty as to where they stand. This situation makes them marginal people.

The Oriental young generation does not want to accept the social norms of its own group. The authoritarian patterns of family life are constantly evaluated against the Ashkenazi family climate. (S1) Unfortunately, the Oriental youth does not have sufficient opportunities to associate with the Ashkenazim in close primary groups, and sometimes he is even rejected in overtly unfriendly ways. (R4) The result is failure to gain any but superficial knowledge of the Ashkenazi culture. The difficulties in acculturation are intensified by tensions in his own family and ethnic community, where parents who are not disposed to change attempt to persuade their children to accept the traditional Oriental patterns of living.

The Oriental youth experiences conflict of motives. He has ambivalent feelings toward membership in his own group: it represents not only threat, but also the satisfaction that goes with membership in a primary group. The large family circle may provide the enjoyment inherent in participation in social functions with people who accept him as an equal, as the dominant Ashkenazi culture does not. The problem is summarized in Newcomb's statement:

> The marginal person's dilemma is that he is motivated toward membership in both more and less favored groups, that each membership carries threats with it, that he cannot have both, and that he cannot give up either. (N2:544)

Marginality is negatively related to family cohesiveness. A noncohesive family breeds marginality, and vice versa. Shannan (S3:113) claims that marginality may lead to waywardness. He found that in many cases the extent of marginality is greater among the younger boys than among their older brothers, and is manifested in a higher frequency of juvenile delinquency among the younger brothers. These findings support the hypothesis developed in this chapter. The older brothers grew up in a relatively more cohesive family and ethnic group. Their family was able to give them sufficient guidance and security and served as a center for moral identification. The younger brothers were much less fortunate. They grew up in families and ethnic communities which were being rocked to their foundation by the giant forces set in motion by contact with Western civilization. Under such pressures the family could not give the youngsters a feeling of security and belongingness. The result was marginality and, in more extreme cases, waywardness.

The impact of the cultural contact between the two groups on the self concept of the Oriental child, on his attitude toward others, and especially on his attitude toward his own group is described in a study by Sapir. (S1) During the floods in the year 1951, 151 Oriental children (from four to fourteen years of age), living with their parents in camps, were transferred to Ashkenazi families. Social workers, visiting the foster homes in order to study the adjustment problems, found that all the Oriental children tried to imitate and incorporate into themselves Ashkenazi modes of behavior. For instance, one girl imitated the food and dress habits of her Ashkenazi girl friend, even to the point of rejecting Oriental food. Many of these children were not used to a bath or shower; most of them, however, made every effort to adjust to these requirements and even went to extremes in their attempts to be clean and polished, and to look like Ashkenazim. These feats of blind imitation were accompanied by a clear rejection by these children of their past background and their families. For instance, one child left the table when Oriental food was served, and many children ignored their parents when the latter visited them dressed in ethnic costumes. Sixty-nine of the 151 children in this study said frankly that they did not want to return to their parents; and this was not so much because of the parents' poverty as because of the authoritarian climate and the domination of the father. Some of the children rejected peers in their own ethnic group and wanted to play only with Ashkenazi children, saying: "When I grow up, I'm going to be an Ashkenazi." (S1:11)

The imitation of the new environment, the rejection of past traditions and of parents, and the almost complete lack of any rebellion against the new demands, show the complexity of the crisis with which the Oriental child is confronted. Sapir says:

> In this experiment the Oriental children paid a very high price emotionally. They developed inferiority feelings, and lost their respect for their families and for the value system of their ethnic group. (S1:36)

Eisenstadt's studies of new immigrants in Israel (E5) differentiate between two types of families—the "solidary" and the "non-solidary." The second type is characterized by lack of cooperation, by constant complaints and mutual accusation for non-fulfillment of economic aspirations, and by disrespect toward the parents (especially the father) who failed to climb the social ladder. The "solidary" family is characterized by the opposite attributes. "A very high correlation has been found between positive predisposition to change and membership in a solidary family, and negative predisposition to change and a non-solidary family." (E5:16) This correlation needs a brief explanation.

A serious cause of distress to many immigrants is the lowering of their social status in the new country. (J1) The emotional security in a solidary family helps its members to overcome this status insecurity and the feeling of social failure. Characterized by high group morale, the solidary family is ready to adjust to the present conditions, and gradually accept some of the new social norms. The non-solidary family evinces a low degree of group morale and rejects any modifications in its modes of behavior. (E5)

Needed Research

It is difficult to generalize about the "average" Oriental family, for two main reasons: (1) There are more than a score of Oriental groups in Israel, and they differ in their customs, outlook, cohesiveness, and similarity to the Ashkenazi culture. (2) All the Oriental groups are in a stage of flux and change. Family life patterns will differ within an ethnic group according to degree of exposure to the Ashkenazi culture. In other words, the family life pattern of a group which immigrated to Israel twenty or thirty years ago will be different from the family life pattern of those who arrived three years ago.

There is need for systematic study of these *various groups in their different stages of development*. In studying these groups the research worker has to look for the significance of the following three important facts in connection with the Oriental family: (1) All the Orientals in Israel are members of a minority group in terms of numbers—constituting 42 per cent of the population (C2)—and also in terms of the possession of power. (2) Most of the Orientals belong to the lower class. (T6) (3) The majority of the Orientals are new immigrants.

An important unexplored area is the *child-rearing practices of the various groups*. (F2) Dynamic theory of personality emphasizes the impact of child-rearing practices on the pattern of the individual's behavior. (E14) Modern anthropology tries to determine how child-rearing practices are related to the basic personality of a culture. For the reader of Hebrew, there is a comprehensive survey of these studies in Avnon's article "New Trends in Psychology." (A5)

In a study entitled "Social Status and Child Rearing Practices" Ericson tested the hypothesis that

> Since different social classes represent different learning environment for children, systematic differences in child rearing practices could be found. A secondary problem of the investigation was to study the effects of training procedures on the development of personality. (E15:494)

> The results of this investigation show that middle class families were generally found to be more exacting in their expectations for children with reference to the learning of habits, cleanliness, training, environmental exploration and control, and age and sex roles. Training was generally begun earlier in the middle class than in the lower class families. In the middle class families, there was more emphasis on the early assumption of responsibility for the self, closer supervision of children's activities and greater emphasis on individual achievement. (E15:498)

> Middle class children are taught ways of living that will prepare them to become financially independent, to assume positions of responsibility in the home and community. (E15:501)

A study by Allison Davis and associates (D3:13–17) reaches similar conclusions, in regard to the impact of the class culture (and especially the family) on the individual. And in another study, Davis says:

> The middle status family uses pressures and goals which build anxiety. The child is taught by a well defined and relatively severe training to strive for . . . a higher age or school, or social class status. . . . Even at the infant level before the age of two years, persistent punishment or disapproval, or other means of arousing shame, guilt, or anxiety are employed systematically to establish weaning and cleanliness, and respect for adults and for property. In adolescence the middle class white child was guided, controlled, supervised by his parents . . . with regard to the following behavior: the time and etiquette of eating, use of the house and car, . . . selection of his social clique, economic matters, attendance at motion pictures, school lessons, grades, and deportment, together with many other areas of control to which adolescents of the lowest status are not subject in their family relationships. (D2:149)

The difference in anxiety and motivation between the two social classes is a key to the understanding of their behavior and is of special importance for the understanding of the lower-class child at school. Testing of these hypotheses among the various Oriental and Ashkenazi groups will contribute toward better understanding of the ethnic problem in Israel, which is highly correlated with a social class stratification.

Other important aspects of the Oriental family that need further research are the following:

The changing role of the father and mother.

Areas of conflict and satisfaction at home.

The marginality conflicts.

Sibling relations.

The place of the adolescent.

The expectations parents have for their children, and their attitudes toward schooling, vocational training, and work.

Aggression and sex mores.

Cultural customs, celebrations, habits of nutrition and hygiene.

Standard of living.

Differences between integrated and disintegrated Oriental families.

Research might lead to a better understanding of, and more sensitivity to, the problems of the Orientals, and to a sincere and a systematic attempt to alleviate these problems. The above-mentioned aspects are suggested for a diagnostic or survey type of research which aims to analyze a specific problem. Another type of research which aims at reduction of ethnic tension, or raising the standard of living of the Oriental family, will be discussed in other chapters.

Summary

The major points discussed in this chapter may be summarized as follows:

1. The contact between the Ashkenazim and the Orientals causes tension, and sometimes even disintegration, in the Oriental family.

2. The cultural contact leads to marginality among the Oriental young generation, and there is a danger of intensification of this marginality in the coming generation.

3. Marginality is negatively related to family cohesiveness.

4. Family non-cohesiveness and marginality are negatively related to positive adjustment and social integration.

5. An important responsibility of education is to build solidarity in the Oriental family.

6. Research is needed on various aspects of the Oriental family.

Nothing was said in this chapter about Ashkenazi families. In general these are relatively harmonious and suffer only from the "normal" conflicts between children and parents. There is relatively complete agreement between the two Ashkenazi generations as to the meaning of life, desired modes of behavior, and symbols of success.

The Ashkenazi family in Israel was never confronted with the same problems as the Oriental one. This fact may be understood only in the light of the difference between the two groups in motivation for immigration. The Ashkenazim have a secular conception of Jewish nationality, and consequently their main objective in coming to Israel was social and cultural reconstruction. The Orientals, on the other hand, "have a traditional conception of Jewish nationality and consequently their main aim was to preserve their existing traditions and customs." (E8:165)

There are some similarities between the problem of the Ashkenazi family of the last generation in the Diaspora (emancipation from extreme Orthodoxy and patriarchal relations) and the problems of the present-generation Oriental family. Warner's analysis of the Jewish family in Yankee City (W2) is helpful in clarifying these similarities.

VIII

Oriental Youth and the Community

THE AVERAGE ORIENTAL CHILD FINDS IT DIFFICULT TO IDEN-
tify with his parents, who deviate from the social norms accepted by
the dominant Ashkenazi culture. On the other hand, he also finds it
difficult to identify with the modern way of life. There are many interrelated circumstances which make this identification difficult or even
impossible. One important factor has already been discussed—the ambivalent feelings of the Oriental child toward membership in his own
group. Membership in this group represents not only a threat but also
the appeal of acceptance in a primary group.

Also important in explaining the difficulties of the Oriental child in
acquiring the modern value system is the fact that he does not have
sufficient opportunities of association with the Ashkenazim in close primary groups. It is this factor that is to be analyzed in this chapter.

As Davis says, "A child can learn a particular culture and a particular moral system only from those people who know this behavior and
who exhibit it in frequent relationships with the learner." (D3:10)
That is, he learns his basic culture and mode of behavior through such
social activities as playing, visiting, and eating and drinking with others.
Consequently the culture of a child is similar to the culture of his social
clique. (D2)

The crucial question is: Does the Oriental child associate intimately
only with the Orientals, and consequently learn only their culture?
There are not sufficient research data to answer this question. This
writer, however, would tend to answer it in the affirmative.

In discussing this question, one must remember that the overwhelm-

65

ing majority of the Orientals belong to the lower class, while the overwhelming majority of the Ashkenazim belong to the middle class. Studies made in the United States show that

> the actual association groups of most Americans are rather severely class limited. This is not meant to suggest that most of them never encounter members of class groups other than their own. But their Primary Groups, those in which they spend most of their time and which usually mean most to them, rarely spread over more than one or two class levels. (N2:563)

An analysis of the basic social institutions in Israel reveals similar conditions. The school will be analyzed in Chapter X. In this chapter, the following institutions will be analyzed in terms of their ethnic composition and extent of inter-ethnic association, and in terms of the role the Oriental youth plays in them: (1) the family; (2) the neighborhood; (3) the synagogue; (4) the youth movement; (5) the club; (6) the coffeehouse; (7) the movies; and (8) the Army.

The Family

Polack says:

> Because of differences in way of living and in cultural traditions there are very few intermarriages between the Ashkenazim and the Orientals. A survey conducted in 1939 showed that families formed by the marriage of an Ashkenazi male to an Oriental female (mainly Sephardi) constituted only one per cent of Ashkenazi families in Jerusalem. (P5:38)

There are no recent data on this subject—a fact easily understood in the light of the taboo that to some extent still surrounds the ethnic issue. The general impression is that: (1) there are very few intermarriages between the two ethnic groups; (2) when these occur they are mainly between the Ashkenazim and the Sephardim; (3) these intermarriages are mainly between Ashkenazi men and Sephardi women; (4) a member of the Oriental middle class, especially a professional person, is more likely to marry an Ashkenazi than is a lower-class Oriental.

In the measurement of social distance, intermarriage is considered the highest index of social proximity. (B7) We assume that a social distance scale in Israel would show a high degree of lip service to the desirability of intermarriage and the readiness of the Israeli citizen for it. In practice, however, this professed national aspiration has not yet been translated into the language of action.

This means that very few Oriental children have Ashkenazi relatives, with whom they can associate intimately, on a kinship basis, and thus learn their mode of behavior.

The Ethnic Neighborhood

The question of ethnic neighborhoods has already been discussed in the chapter on economic differences, the conclusion being that today almost every Israeli city is divided into the "right and wrong sides of the tracks." This division coincides with the ethnic division into Ashkenazi and Oriental neighborhoods. The fact that the majority of Oriental immigrants were housed in deserted Arab villages and towns only makes the division more definite. For instance, a study by Koren (K7) shows that from 87 settlements, established in the year 1949–50 by the Moshav movement, none consisted of a mixed population of Orientals and Ashkenazim.

For the average Oriental child, this means that he does not have many opportunities of association with Ashkenazim in his own neighborhood. This is true only with regard to the many lower-class, not to the few middle-class, Orientals.

> Thus the pivotal meaning of social classes to the student of behavior is that they limit and pattern the learning environment, and they structure the social maze in which the child learns his habits and meanings. (D3:10)

The Synagogue

The synagogue is the castle of isolation of the ethnic groups. It is not only divided according to the two major ethnic groups, but the Oriental synagogue itself is subdivided into many sections: Sephardic, Yemenite, Kurdistan, and so forth. (P5:12) Naturally these ethnic synagogues do not serve as a place for the meeting together of the youth of various communities.

In recent years there have been a few attempts to experiment with a common worship service accepted by the major groups. It is too early to tell how these experiments will affect the situation.

There is a need for research to find out to what extent the ethnic synagogue plays a role in the life of the youth and to what extent it serves as a barrier to intermarriage and to other forms of association.

The impression is that the importance of the ethnic synagogue in the life of the youth is gradually decreasing. Religious and non-religious persons will of course differ in their evaluation of this process. Even the latter, however, must be fully aware of the danger of "redemption from religion" that is not accompanied by identification with another value system. It may lead the Oriental youth toward "negative freedom." (F11)

The various Oriental synagogues are the "forgotten institutions" in the Israeli culture. There is almost no attention given to them in newspapers, magazines, or current books. There is an urgent need for creation of a rapport between the various educational agencies and the ethnic synagogue. The educational agencies should explore the positive potentialities of the ethnic synagogue for the education of the youth.

The Youth Movement

The aspirations of the Zionist movement found their fullest expression in the boys and girls of the youth movement. They exemplify the task-oriented individual whose physical and spiritual energies had to be mobilized always toward the achievement of the national goal. Rieger says:

> The youth movement in its Israeli expression is an heroic and romantic epic. The youth movement was enriched and nurtured by the national ideology of Zionism, by the aspiration for social reform of the Russian Jew, and by the tradition of self improvement of the Galizian immigrants. . . . The collective settlement became for the youth movement the symbol of fulfillment and realization of the most noble national, social, moral, and romantic dreams. (R3:147–48)

The youth movements see their national mission as leaving the convenient urban life and going to cultivate the desert, dry the swamps, and build new settlements in the most dangerous spots.

This brief description shows that the youth movements are composed of the "strong" and selected elite who are ready for self-sacrifice; they are not movements of the "weak"—the masses. Consequently the Israeli youth movements have always been composed of a selected elite, never gaining the actual participation of even the majority of Ashkenazi and claiming even fewer of the Oriental youth. At present, 10 per cent of the Israeli youth are members of the youth movements. (I3:157) The sad fact is that, despite the attempts to recruit more youth from the Orientals, "in most of these movements the number of Orientals is very much smaller than the number of Ashkenazim." (E6:25) In other words, the youth movement does not serve as a meeting ground for the intimate and close association of the average Oriental and Ashkenazi youth.

The idealistic goals of the youth movement do not appeal to many sectors of the Oriental youth. Says an Oriental leader:

> Pioneering Zionism, with all its self-sacrificing demands, is of interest to the middle-class intellectual youth (mainly Ashkenazi). The children of the poor families (Orientals) want to taste some of the earthly pleasures which surround them in the cities—nice apartments, European suits . . . (Y1:10)

Both the extreme idealistic goals of the youth movement and the content and structure of its activities make the participation of the Oriental youth very difficult. In abstract discussions about various political and social questions, which demand high verbal ability and much information, the relatively not so well informed and the less capable in verbal expression are at a disadvantage.

The activities of the youth movement are highly structured and consequently demand much group discipline. The movement is divided into small groups, each of which in most cases moves as a whole from one activity to another. The individual cannot change freely from activity to activity or from group to group. In such a structure the participant has to be well disciplined and ready to give up his individual interests.

Even the recreational activities of the youth movement have a national and task-oriented character. The only dances allowed are Israeli folk dances; ballroom dancing is tabooed. The sports are mainly of a martial nature—preparation for the national need of defense. There is a planned de-emphasizing of the "non-productive" sports, such as football, basketball, etc., and neglect of the cultivation of individual hobbies. In short, the whole program is directed toward the preparation of the task-oriented pioneer.

At present the overwhelming majority of the Oriental youth are not ready to participate in and enjoy these activities. Two major reasons are lack of the pioneer motivation and lack of ability of the required kinds.

The youth movements have never been fully aware of these difficulties or of the need to "meet the Orientals where they are." The youth movement must learn to adapt its program to the present interests and abilities of the average child—and especially of the Oriental child. For instance, it could build on the skill and eagerness these children display in their ball games and other non-structured and non-directed activities.

The adaptation of the program also means the modification of the ego ideal. Even the concept of pioneering is interpreted too narrowly—mainly as building a new settlement. There is an urgent need to broaden this concept and interpret pioneering as citizenship awareness and alertness both in the community and outside of it. The Israeli educator must face the statistical fact that very few of the youth will leave the city and become farmer pioneers. All of them, however, will become citizens and consequently have to learn to work on the problems facing their own communities.

The one-sided interpretation of the concept of pioneering is illustrated in a speech by Atzmon, one of the leaders of the Gadna movement. Speaking before a recent conference of the Israeli High School Association (I3), he suggested the establishing of a model autonomic youth state in the Negev, to be called "Well of Light," for the purpose of citizenship and pioneering education. This proposal, however dynamic, illustrates the prevalent trend of thinking, which sees training for a national task as going outside of the city and away from the real masses. (F3)

The youth movement will be much more appealing to the Oriental youth *and to their parents* if part of its activities are directed into sensitizing the youth to the everyday problems confronting them in the community, the ethnic group, and the family and into showing them how they can help in making their own community a better place to live in.

Changing the program in this direction will open a new area for cooperation between the youth movement on the one hand and the Oriental parents and leaders on the other. At present there is almost no contact between the two parties.

The Oriental parent, characterized by a low predisposition toward

change, has an apathetic or negative attitude toward the youth movement. The fact that this social institution is new and foreign partly
explains this attitude. The crusading and indoctrinating spirit of the
movement only intensifies this attitude.

> Instead of capitalizing on the present attachment of the Yemenite youth
> to the traditional Jewish culture, and on their attitude of devotion to
> the country—instead of building further education on this existing basis
> —there is a tendency to ignore the potentialities of these values, to
> destroy the traditional symbols, and to start from the beginning.
> (R4:280)

This revolutionary approach is a source of tension between the youth
movement and the Oriental community which identifies partly or wholly
with the symbols of the past. This negating approach sometimes
creates a transitional stage of non-belonging to the traditional culture
on the one hand and non-identification with the modern culture on the
other. This transitional stage can result in the intensification of the
dangerous conditions of anomie.

The youth movement may be proud of many of its achievements in
destroying completely or almost completely the ethnic barriers between
its Ashkenazi and Oriental members. This success supports the theory
which claims that working together on a common problem and participation on an equal basis is the basic approach to the solution of the
ethnic conflict. (W3) In spite of these encouraging facts, a serious
number of young Orientals are hesitating, consciously or unconsciously,
to join the youth movement, having a feeling of social distance and
strangeness in a predominantly Ashkenazi group.

The task-oriented member of the youth movement is educated to
think in terms of national ideals and values. He does not, however,
have the needed training in terms of sensitivity to human relationships.
He is a task-oriented and not a personal-oriented individual. (F3)

There are many problems of human relationship involved in activities
which include adolescents from two diverse ethnic and socio-economic
backgrounds. The lower-class Oriental adolescent may feel a little
awkward and hesitant in his behavior, especially in his relationships
with the other sex. The Oriental boy feels that he is not welcomed by
the Ashkenazi girl as the Ashkenazi boy is. The Oriental girl yearns
for an Ashkenazi boy friend when she is thirteen to sixteen years old,
but later "matures" and becomes "realistic."

The task-oriented members of the youth movement must recognize these problems. Only an education which stresses awareness of and sensitivity to human relationships can help the adolescents of the two diverse backgrounds to overcome the social distance and ethnic strangeness which exist at present.

The opportunities of the two youth groups to associate together under the common roof of the youth movement are limited by another important factor. Many of the youth are divided into the Working Youth (Noar Oved) and the School Youth (Noar Lomed). Automatically this division results in *de facto* segregation of two economic strata, since most of the Orientals are in fact working and so naturally belong to the Working Youth group.

Despite the fact that the Oriental youth are a minority even in the Working Youth movement, the inner division of this organization, according to neighborhood location, creates a situation where in some centers almost one hundred per cent of the participants are Oriental youth. In other words, the division into Working Youth and School Youth and the inner division of the Working Youth into neighborhood centers were made without sufficient consideration of the importance of mutual participation of youth from the two ethnic groups.

Another example which illustrates the same point is the inner division of the Boy Scout movement in Jerusalem. This organization is divided into four branches. Three of these branches draw their membership from private schools (elementary and high schools) and only one of the branches (called the Kehila) draws its membership from the regular public schools. According to an unofficial report, the Kehila is composed almost entirely of Orientals, while in the others the percentage of Orientals is almost zero.

These illustrations point not to any policy of ethnic segregation but to the tragic mistakes of overlooking the crucial importance of mutual ethnic association and of failing to realize that certain convenient administrative procedures might result in some *de facto* ethnic segregation.

In general, the youth movement can be proud of many of its achievements in educating the Oriental youth and in integrating the youth of the two ethnic groups. The following modifications will make this institution a most constructive factor in the improvement of ethnic group relations: broadening the concept of the ego ideal, individualization of the program, cooperation with the Oriental community, greater emphasis on the problem of human relationship, and an administrative structure based on mutual ethnic association.

The Club

The formal ethnic association for young people plays an important role in perpetuating the culture of its own group and in maintaining its cohesiveness. In describing the Greek community in Yankee City, Warner says:

> The G.A.P.A. [a formal ethnic association of Greek adults] established the junior auxiliary for these purposes: 1) to organize formally the boys' recreation; 2) to articulate the boys into the Greek community system and conversely to keep them from disassociating themselves from the community; 3) to subordinate the boys formally to the controls of their fathers, who are organized in the senior G.A.P.A., e.g., by means of the adviser to the juniors. (W2:280)

This is an illustration of a deliberate and planned attempt on the part of the adults to help the youth find its place within its culture and prevent disintegration.

The battered Oriental Jewish community in Israel has not established such organizations for its youth, mainly because of the disintegration of its communal life. As a result of this disintegration the Oriental community lost its power and role as a guide in the activities of the younger generation. In many cases, the parents and the community exert some influence in preventing the youth from joining certain organizations (such as the youth movement); in only rare cases do they have a positive guiding influence.

The dissolution of the ties between the young Orientals and the senior ethnic organization is strongly felt. The youth rarely look for assistance from the ethnic charity organizations, and many of them gradually break away from the ethnic synagogue. (F6)

Another important reason for the failure of the Oriental Jews to establish formal junior ethnic associations is the lack of this type of institution among the Ashkenazim—the youth movement and a few sport clubs being the exceptions. In short, there are no traditional patterns of formal youth organization which can be followed by the Oriental youth. This phenomenon is very striking to anyone who tries to study the Israeli culture. It has important implications for the social life and the mental health of all Israeli boys and girls, and especially for the Orientals.

The role of any formal association, as interpreted within the Israeli value system, is to work for fulfillment of a national and social task. The members of a formal association (e.g., the Women's Zionist Organization, WIZO) meet in order to help someone else, such as under-privileged children or the sick. The formal junior organization—the youth movement—gets together in order that the youth may prepare themselves for the national task. The individual is seen in these formal organizations as an instrument and not as an aim. The groups do not meet to plan and work for personal self-improvement, and they have almost no recreational activities.

Clubs are, in general, organizations where people gather mainly for the purpose of recreation, social life, and self-improvement. Unfortunately there is no institution in the Israeli culture which recognizes and supports these purposes. This attitude is reinforced by a similar tradition in the Jewish culture as a whole. A description of the associations of the older Jewish generation in Yankee City shows that "the benefit element is predominant and the recreational element is negligible." (W2:266)

Another reason for the lack of clubs is the organizational structure of the formal senior associations and the few formal junior associations. These social institutions are organized mainly on a centralized national basis. To illustrate: almost every community has a WIZO, J.N.F. (Jewish National Fund), or Working Youth association, directed by and connected to some central committee. There are hardly any "grass roots" associations of small groups of people who meet together for a certain cause and are not connected to, and directed by, a central National Committee. The cultural pattern is characterized by an overemphasis on the big organization and by de-emphasizing the small group. (F3) The result is that there has been little development of small, self-directed groups such as clubs.

The above analysis shows some of the major reasons for the almost complete absence of clubs in the Israeli culture. (The youth movement is an exception.) For the Oriental youth this means intensification of the conditions of anomie.

The Board of Education and some non-political organizations have attempted in recent years to establish clubs and playgrounds for children. These facilities, however, are mainly reserved for the elementary school children. The Oriental adolescents lack this framework, which provides positive and constructive forms of recreation.

The stress of marginality and anomie is especially acute during adolescence. The life of the Oriental adults is structured by job and family responsibilities; the life of the Oriental children is structured by school, family supervision, and play in close neighborhood peer groups. Denied these conditions, the Oriental adolescent is left in a cultural vacuum. The adolescent works part of the week and then loiters around aimlessly with his gang, without a constructive outlet for his energy or a creative way to spend his leisure hours.

Sociologically speaking, the Oriental adolescent presents a unique problem—he lives in an "adolescent phase" but lacks an "adolescent culture." Goitine (G2) describes in detail the continuous and cohesive structure of the individual in Yemen, where there is no gap or transition period between the life of the child and the adult life. The boy participates in adult activities in the synagogue, and helps the father in his job. In other words, there was almost no adolescent stage of development in the life of the Jew in Yemen, and consequently there was no need for a development of an adolescent culture.

In Israel, under the impact of the modern Ashkenazi civilization, the postponement of the marriage age, the secularization and individuation processes, and the prolonged preparation for economic independence, there has emerged a formal adolescent stage of development, lacking, however, a meaningful adolescent culture and content.

> The Yemenite adolescent [in Israel] does not have many opportunities for social and recreational activities or much provision for spiritual growth which might become the basis for the development of social ideals. (R4:272)

A vicious circle is created: the lack of an enriching adolescent culture results in purposeless loitering, and vice versa. Only a radical change in the way of life of the Oriental youth will save them and the whole Oriental community from anomie and stagnation. The encouragement of club activities that figure importantly in their pattern of living is a step toward this needed change.

For the improvement of ethnic group relations, it is desirable that each club be composed of the members of both major communities. In practice, however, this membership structure will, in some cases, not be possible because of ecological structure, social distance, or differences in interests. In these cases, it is the task of the educator to help in the establishment of clubs even if only on a purely ethnic basis.

Under sympathetic leadership, free of political domination, these purely ethnic clubs might become a springboard for mutual association with the other ethnic groups. In Yankee City, the ethnic junior association had an important reconstructive role.

> Rather than react against both sets of elements [American and ethnic], or against only the ethnic element in his personality, the child may come to reconcile both—he may join others in his ethnic group to form an association whose symbols are partly American and partly ethnic. (W2:147)

In the club the ethnic youth will find a sense of belongingness, security, status, and a sense of direction which will make it easier for them to reconstruct their own value system and modes of behavior. This transitional stage will prepare them to meet and join the Ashkenazi youth, *as a group*. In these circumstances the Oriental youth will be able not only to receive passively from and be influenced by the Ashkenazim, but also to contribute to and change the Ashkenazi culture. The improvement of ethnic group relations will be served through "a melting pot which fuses its diverse ethnic elements into a new amalgam," rather than by "a system which performs the transmutation of diverse ethnic elements into elements almost homogeneous with its own." (W2:155)

Reciprocal give-and-take relations, under the auspices of a club, will enhance the morale of the Oriental youth and destroy the walls of prejudice, suspicion, and fear, and eliminate the superiority-inferiority feelings which at the present separate the two groups.

The Coffeehouse and the Movies

There is need for research into the type of activities in which the Oriental youth are engaged during their leisure time. Observation is sufficient to show, however, that two common media of recreation are coffeehouses and movies. These institutions certainly keep the youth "out of mischief," yet they do not contribute toward the improvement and enrichment of their lives.

The characteristic conditions of attendance at the cinema and the coffeehouse are anonymity and relative passivity. (E6) The problem of the Oriental youth is one of belongingness and purposefulness. The movies and the coffeehouse keep the Oriental youth in an anonymous status where he does nothing to recreate his own life and to achieve a sense of belongingness and direction.

These two institutions, in fact, only aggravate the conditions and intensify the tensions in the Oriental youth by presenting to him a luxurious Western pattern of living which he will never be able to achieve. The strong identification with the movie world creates a dichotomy in the life of many Orientals—identification with the film stars' way of living on the one hand and actual spiritual and economic poverty on the other. Neither the movies nor the coffeehouses provide any plan for bridging the gap between these two separate worlds. No wonder that students of juvenile delinquency consider movies to be important among the forces that promote delinquency. (F7)

In the movie houses the Oriental youth meets the Ashkenazi youth on the most superficial level—they are sitting together in the same hall. This association does not contribute toward closer relationship and does not serve as a basis for learning a new mode of behavior.

In the coffeehouse, the average Oriental youth sits and chats with members of his own ethnic clique. Despite the absence of any official policy of segregation, in coffeehouses, a "gentlemen's agreement" atmosphere, differences in prices and locations, and, in some cases, years' old "traditions" tend to establish many coffeehouses as meeting places for distinct groups and consequently create some *de facto* segregation.

Research is needed to find out the extent of the association of Oriental and Ashkenazi youth in the same coffeehouses, and the degree of intimacy of this association.

The Army

The Israeli Army is one of the most powerful and promising educational institutions in the country. It has unique potentialities for bringing the youth of the two ethnic communities to share the same experiences and cooperate for a common cause.

The Army professes and attempts to practice the principle of equality of opportunity for everyone, regardless of ethnic or class origin. It succeeds more than any other Israeli institution in bringing the youth of the various ethnic groups into close association. Its success is limited, however, by the lack of a planned program for ethnic group relationship. This stems from the fact that there is almost no awareness of the existence of ethnic tensions or of the potential of the Army for alleviating those tensions. Some areas of ethnic conflict which are overlooked or ignored by the Army will be analyzed here.

The Oriental youth are very sensitive to the fact that they live in a world which is ruled by the Ashkenazi. In the Army they are confronted with an even more pronounced manifestation of Ashkenazi dominance, being, in most cases, commanded by Ashkenazi officers. There are no statistics on the ethnic composition of the officer corps, but it is a matter of common knowledge that the number of Orientals is very limited.

The Army, trying to be objective and scientific, recommends soldiers for officers' schools on the basis of psychotechnical examinations, mainly verbal and non-verbal intelligence tests. These tests, being culturally loaded, discriminate against the new-immigrant and lower-class Orientals and do not provide them with an equal chance of competing with the Ashkenazim.

High intelligence is only one qualification of a good officer. Speaking of "officer material," Yadin, the Israeli chief of staff, mentioned many personality traits such as leadership, stability, and devotion. (I3) In practice, however, the private is recommended for officers' school mainly on the basis of his score on a so-called intelligence battery. The result is another failure to give Oriental youth a chance to climb the social ladder.

Army life and organization have many unpalatable facets which may easily be interpreted by some Orientals as marks of Ashkenazi superiority and dominance. The Army is based on autocratic relations, social distance, emphasis on status symbols, and privileges for the higher ranks which the private will not ignore. When these are accompanied by an ethnic stratification, a "psychology" of ethnic discrimination may develop.

Only an immediate and planned endeavor of training Oriental youth to become officers may stop the development of the "psychology" of ethnic preference which is at present only in its early stages. The establishment of a stratum of Oriental officers will renew the belief of the Oriental youth in the existence of equality of opportunity. The Oriental officers will become a center of identification for the Oriental youth. They will constitute an important motivational factor for efforts of social advancement and promotion, not only in the Army but also in the country as a whole.

Another area of ethnic tension and prejudice which is overlooked by Army authorities is that of inter-ethnic relationships between the sexes. The Israeli army drafts boys and girls who are eighteen years of age or older. One of the major characteristics of this age is interest in the opposite sex. In contrast to the Israeli adolescent, whose heterosexual interest is expressed in *group* relations between the two sexes, in this young adulthood age there is a serious development of relations on an individual basis—going out in couples as compared to group entertainment, ballroom dances versus group folk dances, and "going steady" as against casual friendships.

In this crucial phase of development, then, the *bulk* of Ashkenazi and Oriental youth meet socially together under the auspices of the Army. Unfortunately, however, Army life has in it many elements which are not conducive, and may even be detrimental, to the development of healthy relationships between the sexes. Male and female soldiers are segregated into different camps, and contact between them is controlled and regimented. An atmosphere of suspicion and mistrust prevails—expressed often even in lectures of senior officers to the female soldiers, advising them to "beware" of the male soldiers, and intensified by a public opinion of some conservative groups who object "on moral grounds" to the drafting of girls.

Obviously, this atmosphere is not conducive to overcoming the social distance and suspicion which already exist between Oriental girls and Ashkenazi boys, and between Ashkenazi girls and Oriental boys. It makes them hesitant and awkward in getting acquainted and solidifies present practices that tend to establish social segregation. Here is another conclusive proof of that cardinal principle that ethnic group relationships constitute an integral part of the total human relations atmosphere.

Improvement of relations between the sexes in the Army is a prerequisite for the achievement of healthier relations between boys and girls of different ethnic groups. The Army needs a program of constructive activities which will bring the two ethnic groups and the two sexes together to work on common projects, such as clubs, committees, study groups, dances, and trips. The democratization of the Army through greater freedom of choice, delegation of more planning and decision-making to the private soldier, and a relaxation of the prevailing rigidity in the pattern of organization, will create a wider field of action for the soldiers and will allow closer association between the two sexes in planning and execution of programs.

It is hoped that the democratization of the Army will result in a high group morale which will in turn create better ethnic group relations. This "indirect approach," however, is not sufficient. It is only a first step, which has to be followed by a *direct* attack on the manifestations of prejudice and social distance, including the relegation of the Oriental soldier to lower positions in the Army. This will require (1) a deliberate attempt to bring the youth of the two ethnic groups into close association and to help them to belong to the same primary group, and (2) a frank and realistic discussion of all the aspects of this problem in the Army (including the problem of relations between the sexes) and in the country as a whole.

Another point which needs clarification is the problem of drafting Oriental girls into the Army. The drafting of girls into the Army has been one of the most controversial issues in the country. The draft is opposed mainly by the religious conservative elements of the population. The law now grants the right of exemption from Army service to girls who find it objectionable "on religious grounds." There are no statistics to show the effect of this provision on the number of Oriental girls entering the Army. One may assume that more of the Oriental than of the Ashkenazi girls take advantage of this provision. The result is a smaller proportion of Oriental girls in the Army.

Army experience can be one of the most constructive factors in the education of deprived Oriental girls, and for many of them the Army is the first and major step in emancipation from the patriarchal family. It helps them to integrate and identify with the democratic value system of the Israeli culture. At the same time, however, the Army is a frightening and bewildering experience for some of the Oriental girls, and it probably accentuates the tension between them and their traditional families.

The liberal elements in the Israeli public should be made fully aware of these conflicts. There is need for educational enterprises which will bridge the gap of centuries now separating the patriarchal family from the modern Army, with regard to drafting of girls. There is need for an organization that will prepare the Oriental family in general and Oriental youth in particular (especially the girls) for Army life.

At present the Gadna (pre-Army youth units) tries to achieve some of these goals by preparing the Israeli adolescent for Army life. In practice, however, the activities of this organization are not broad enough; many of the Oriental boys and the majority of the Oriental girls take no part. There is an urgent need for a militant program which will increase the number of Oriental youth in the Gadna. This could be achieved only by establishing more rapport and working cooperatively with the Oriental parents and the Oriental community as a whole.

Preparation of the Oriental boys and girls, and of their parents, for their future Army life will make this life a much more educative experience.

Discussion of this topic would not be complete without some mention of the ethnic group problem in the Hagana, the predecessor of the Israeli Army and the "official underground" of the Jewish community of Palestine.

Past experience in the Hagana, especially in its mobilized units, the Palmakh, shows that when Oriental and Ashkenazi youth live in the same camp, belong to the same platoon, and work for a common cause, the barriers of ethnic strangeness disappear. This is encouraging evidence that the ethnic conflict can be resolved. This experience points to the basic approach to the resolution of the ethnic problem—participation with equal status, working together on a common cause.

Despite its above-mentioned success, the Hagana, too, failed in mobilizing a sufficient representation of the Oriental youth, especially of the Oriental girls. Selective factors similar to those which operate in the youth movements also operated in the Hagana: monopolization and dominance by the middle-class culture, membership composed mainly of Ashkenazi youth, the resistance of parents, and so forth. The Israeli public was never made fully aware of the disproportionate representation, and there was never any deliberate large-scale attempt to raise the number of Oriental youth in the Hagana, or to adapt its activities to their needs and interests.

Effects of Segregation

This chapter has brought out the prevalence of some *de facto* segregation in the major institutions of the Israeli community. This situation has profound effects on the Israeli youth, especially the young Oriental.

For the Oriental youth, segregation means lack of opportunity to learn the culture and mode of behavior of the Ashkenazim. Since the young Oriental is a marginal person whose "reference group" is the Ashkenazi culture, this leads to conditions of anomie, and individual and group maladjustment.

For the Oriental youth, segregation also means a lack of opportunity to *change* the Ashkenazi culture and mode of behavior—lack of opportunity to create, together with the Ashkenazim, a new culture based on the value systems of both groups.

This synthetic culture would give the young Oriental a sense of active partnership and a sense of belongingness. Being a giver and not only a receiver would raise his status and bolster his morale. A feeling of partnership in building a new culture would result in less ethnic defensiveness and in better ethnic group relations.

Progress toward this goal of a synthesized culture, with all its social and psychological concomitants, is severely hampered by the present prevalence of partial segregation.

Another basic effect of the limited opportunities for mutual and close association between ethnic groups is the creation of some feelings of prejudice. A vicious circle is created: segregation, leading to prejudice, creates in turn more segregation.

The interrelationship between segregation and prejudice has been observed by many students of ethnic group problems in America. Brameld says:

> Where people of various cultures and races genuinely associate, there tensions and difficulties, prejudices and confusions dissolve; where they do not associate, where they are isolated from one another, there prejudice and conflict grow like disease. (B9:245)

The attitudes of prejudice and social distance are a cause for and a product of the ethnic hierarchy in Israel. While these attitudes are mutual, they have a more detrimental effect on the Oriental than on the Ashkenazi youth.

The Oriental child is born into a society arranged in a hierarchy according to ethnic origin. In this hierarchy the Ashkenazi is in the upper echelon. The Oriental community itself has a status hierarchy—from the lowest status, represented by the Kurdim, to the highest status, represented by the Sephardim. (F7) A recent sociometric study (T8) of the relationship among new immigrants shows: (1) the existence of two definite social hierarchies, one among the Ashkenazim and the other among the Orientals; (2) very little contact between these two hierarchies; (3) rejection by other Oriental groups of the Yemenites and the Moroccans.

The Oriental youth is affected by this ethnic hierarchy. He grows up in a shadow cast by his ethnic origin. Gradually he learns that he is a member of an ethnic group considered inferior in its social status. The effect of this is apparent in the Oriental personality, although it is not the most important personality determinant, family and class influences being more important.

Although the attitudes of prejudice are mild and in most cases concealed, the Oriental youth encounters them in many subtle forms. Ormian says: "The lower-class Oriental adolescent feels that the Ashkenazi group despises him, and generally it is true; feelings of inferiority and jealousy hamper his emotional and social development." (O4:39)

In some cases the member of the minority group, becoming bitter and disillusioned, decides he will have nothing to do with the dominant group beyond what is necessary. He may remain in a ghetto inhabited by members of his own group only or he may take out his bitterness in aggressive behavior, with a "chip on his shoulder." Such aggressive behavior is a normal reaction to the frustration he endures in the family and in the community. It has in it, however, the seeds of future disorders that can inhibit growth toward a democratic and healthy society.

Three antisocial phenomena of aggressive behavior, which stem from the frustration endured by the Oriental youth, will be analyzed here: (1) ethnic clashes; (2) juvenile delinquency; (3) the Irgun.

Ethnic Clashes

Speaking about ethnic "incidents," a Yemenite leader says: "Our boys join in defense or attack on every public or private issue between a Yemenite and a member of another ethnic group, without considering whether their side is right or wrong." (Y1:11)

Students of the Oriental group report similar observations of ethnic hostility, which occasionally results in serious incidents. (F7) This type of hostile activity indulged in by the youth of the various ethnic groups (and not only by Orientals against Ashkenazim), should serve as a grave warning. It is unwise to regard these incidents (rare, thus far) as "children's play," or as an "infantile disorder" stage of the young State.

Unless a dynamic program of bringing closer the youth of the various ethnic groups is embarked on, there is danger that in some cases the present hostile attitudes will develop into open ethnic clashes. A few incidents of this kind have already occurred.

Juvenile Delinquency

Studies made in the United States (J1) show that the crime rate among second-generation Americans is higher than the rate among the foreign-born or the native-born Americans of American parentage. (Some cohesive groups are an exception.) Similar results were found in Israel. The second-generation young Orientals make up the bulk of juvenile delinquents in the country. For instance, according to statistics of 1946, more than 90 per cent of the wayward youth in Jerusalem were Orientals. (F7)

Studies of ecological factors in human behavior show that "The most important factor in accounting for the delinquency is the breakdown of the social conditions which maintain normal and conventional behavior in the stable community." (F3:744) The disintegration of the Oriental community, the disruption of family life, lower-class privations, and feelings of ethnic inferiority are major factors, then, in this delinquency of Oriental youth. An inner analysis of the delinquency figures shows that a high rate of juvenile delinquency is positively related to the degree of community disintegration. (F7)

Oriental delinquency is committed mainly in groups, while Ashkenazi delinquency is mainly individualistic. (F9) Gang delinquency is the protest reaction of some juvenile Orientals against a culture which does not provide them with equality of opportunity and status. In the framework of the delinquent gang, the Oriental boy satisfies his needs for recognition, belongingness, and social status which are denied to him by the rejecting dominant group.

The Oriental juvenile delinquency is a group phenomenon and should be dealt with as such. The destructive powers of the juvenile gang have to be redirected into constructive channels. Nadad says:

> No intervention on the part of the educator will be successful in strengthening and enriching the weak ego of a neglected youth, unless the latter is able to orient himself within a *collective framework* which will lay some obligation upon him. He must be given the chance of utilizing the values he has acquired, and of translating them into deeds within such a framework. (N1:5)

In putting these therapeutic principles into practice, the Israeli organizations evince a preference for transferring the "neglected children" from an urban to a rural community. This approach is consistent with the philosophy of the task-oriented Zionist culture, which emphasizes the therapeutic effects of rural life. This approach, however, has many limitations; e.g., it is curative and not preventive, it causes an unhealthy separation of family members, and it pushes the emotionally disturbed youngsters into a pioneering way of life which is tough and hazardous even for mature and idealistic adults.

A much more fruitful and promising approach to the solution of the problem is dealing with the wayward youth in their natural environment—their own communities and families. "The educator has to regard both the neglected youngsters and the environment itself as the object of his educational and social intervention." (N1:4)

The energies of the delinquent gang must be channeled into reconstruction of their own community and neighborhood. The solution for the slum areas is not abandoning them, as the present pioneering ideology calls for; the solution is rebuilding the slums. At present there is almost no social contact between the Oriental youth of the slum areas, which are the major "delinquency areas" (B4), and organized groups of Ashkenazim. Unification with such groups, under the auspices of a socially oriented club, could be a major determinant in building identification with positive social norms and in building self-esteem in these underprivileged youth. From the point of view of solving the juvenile delinquency problem, which is an integral part of the ethnic group question, the importance of such unification cannot be overemphasized.

Speaking about a group of delinquent Oriental boys who appeared in a dramatic play in a youth movement camp, Nadad says:

> The spontaneous applause at the final curtain marked the integration of the wayward boys from Jerusalem into the life of the ordinary youth; it forged a strong link between the youth movement and the boys from the Jerusalem slum. (N1:10)

The Irgun

There are no statistics to show the ethnic composition of the Irgun. However, it is the observation of some writers, both Oriental (Y1) and Ashkenazi (G3), that the part of the Oriental youth in this "dissident underground" was much larger than their part in the Hagana, the "official underground."

The Hagana, with its educational and social activities, did not appeal to and did not succeed in mobilizing the Oriental youth. The fanatic and chauvinistic ideology of the Irgun and its relative lack of social and educational activity had a far greater appeal. In the Irgun some of the Oriental youth found an outlet for their resentment, not only of the British and the Arabs, but also of the governing Ashkenazi institutions.

From the psychological point of view, participation in the Irgun was most important in raising the injured self-esteem of the Oriental boy. It gave him a feeling of belonging to and identification with a great national cause. Unfortunately these actions, which had some positive psychological results, were most destructive socially.

As we look toward the future, there are two major points to be noted in connection with the relatively great participation of the Oriental youth in the Irgun. The first point is very encouraging. The Oriental youth is striving for participation in social institutions. He wants to identify with the national aspirations. There is need for a friendly hand that can direct this desire into socially constructive channels.

The second point, however, is very discouraging. The underprivileged sectors of the Oriental youth are the potential prey of any chauvinistic or totalitarian movement. Their feelings of hostility and aggression, their tendency to identify themselves with political sloganeering

(F7), and their lack of social maturity may be exploited by a future fanatic party.

The element of violence has increased in importance in Israeli politics over the last few years. While in the past this political aggression was directed mainly against a foreign power, the British, today it erupts also in the internal affairs of the country. The unscrupulous activities of some political parties, the use of violent demonstrations, propaganda, and parades which create a mob atmosphere—all these set before the youth a constant example of violence as a way of attacking problems. And the Oriental youth who has never had the experience and tradition of democratic living is especially liable to be influenced by this.

Needed Research

This chapter is based mainly on impressions gained from observation. There is some research on the most acute problems of the Oriental youth, such as waywardness, but there is almost no research on the social development of the average Oriental boy and girl.

A basic hypothesis of this chapter is that the extent of association between average Oriental and Ashkenazi young people is very limited. The writer is fully aware that this hypothesis may arouse the resentment of many Israeli readers; but he believes that further research will show that a problem of some *de facto* segregation in the various community institutions definitely exists.

Such research is needed, for instance, in the following areas:

Analysis of the major social institutions in terms of their ethnic composition and the degree of social proximity within the membership.

Analysis of the ideals, programs, and administrative policies of these institutions in terms of their impact on the ethnic composition and interrelationships.

Modes of behavior of Oriental and Ashkenazi youth.

Modes of behavior of segregated and non-segregated Oriental youth.

Modes of behavior of lower-class and middle-class Oriental youth.

Conditions which hamper or facilitate the cause of mutual association between Oriental and Ashkenazi youth.

The attitudes of Oriental boys, girls, and parents toward the various social institutions.

The relationship between the Oriental youth and his own ethnic community and ethnic organizations. The development of group consciousness and identification in the Oriental child.

Relationships between the youth of the various Oriental ethnic groups.

Relationship between the old-timer young Oriental of a certain ethnic group and the newcomer of the same group.

Summary

An attempt has been made in this chapter to show the existence of some *de facto* segregation in the major institutions of the community. These institutions could be classified in the following order—from most segregated to least segregated: the synagogue, the family, the neighborhood, the youth movement, the coffeehouse, and the Army.

The place of the Oriental youth in these institutions and the opportunities they offer for mutual association of Oriental and Ashkenazi youth have been discussed. The major effects of the limited nature of these opportunities for close association are (1) the intensification of the condition of anomie in which the Oriental youth live and (2) the development of feelings of prejudice.

The chapter discussed the danger of the vicious circle of prejudice-and-segregation and emphasized the importance of mutual ethnic association for the improvement of ethnic group relations. Watson, a proponent of this theory, says:

> If we try to change people's feelings while the caste barriers remain tacitly accepted, the habits built around these barriers will silently undo anything we accomplish. On the other hand, persons with strong prejudices who have to live and work together soon experience human qualities and relationships which tend to break down the prejudice. (W3:64)

It is very difficult to change the established forms of life that create *de facto* segregation among adults; it is much easier, however, to do so among the youth, especially in a nation that is determined to achieve a complete unification of its various ethnic components.

Failure to start a militant program for the abolition of *de facto* segregation among Israeli youth will only aggravate the ethnic problem in the country, solidifying the ethnic barriers and intensifying prejudice and conflicts.

Part Four

THE ETHNIC PROBLEM
AND THE SCHOOL

IX

Oriental Youth and the School

An IMPORTANT ROLE OF THE SCHOOL IS TO SERVE AS A
major channel through which the nation can achieve its social aspiration—the evolution of a unified nation from diversified heterogeneous
elements.

It is the purpose of this chapter to analyze some of the administrative
and curricular principles of the Israeli school in the light of the ethnic
problem. The analysis will show that in spite of great efforts and many
achievements the school has partly failed in its mission of improving
ethnic group relations, and in some cases has even added new ethnic
tensions.

School Segregation

The previous chapter stressed the importance of mutual association
for the improvement of ethnic relations. The educational authorities
in Israel failed to consider this principle in planning school zoning. In
too many cases Ashkenazi and Oriental children have no opportunities
for close association for the simple reason that they do not study in
the same school. Although there is no deliberate policy of school
segregation, many schools are in fact segregated or semi-segregated.

This claim may seem exaggerated, or even insulting, to some Israeli
readers. There is, however, some statistical evidence to prove it. The
following table (E13) shows the ethnic composition of the population
of the elementary schools in Tel Aviv. The total enrollment in this
school system is, approximately, 57 per cent Ashkenazi and 43 per cent
Oriental. (E13)

School	Percentage of Pupils Ashkenazi	Oriental
The Yemenite School	—	100
Ahavat Zion	—	100
Zrubavel	—	100
Hakarmel	96	4
Bamerkaz	95	5
Bilu	95	5
Tel-Nordoi	93	7
Hashmonaim	93	7
Nes-Ziona	92	8
Shlomo-Hamelekh	91	9
Ysod-Hamala	9	91
Frishman	90	10
Nve-Tzedek (M)	10	90
Talpiot	90	10
Balfur	88	12
Ledugma	88	12
Ehad-Haam	84	16
Bialik	28	72
Hashakhar	28	72
Nve-Shanan (M)	28	72
Hatzafon	71	29
Bazel	71	29
Nve-Tzedek (F)	30	70
Yavne	69	31
Sarona	69	31
Gewla	34	66
Nve-Shanan (F)	37	63
Takhkemony	52	48

Assuming that enrollment not exceeding 10 per cent of Ashkenazi or Oriental pupils in a school means *de facto* segregation, the above table shows that 14 of the 28 elementary schools in Tel Aviv are segregated. In 50 per cent of the schools belonging to this system, then, the pupils have little or no opportunity to associate with children of the other ethnic group.

The ecological distribution of the population into ethnic neighborhoods only partly explains this situation. The zoning of the school districts was enacted without any consideration of the ethnic factor. In some cases, the zoning regulations followed already established school districts, partly based on the unspoken principle of "gentlemen's agreement." The children residing on the "wrong side of the tracks"—

mainly Orientals—went to one school, while the children on the "right side"—mainly Ashkenazim—went to the other.

An examination of the school zone map of Tel Aviv shows that some school districts can easily be changed in order to achieve a stronger ethnic association among the pupils.

Lack of mutual ethnic association is much more severe in Jerusalem than in Tel Aviv. There is no system of school zoning in Jerusalem. The parent has the right to send his child to any elementary school in the city. The result is a high degree of school segregation. There is in force an unspoken "gentlemen's agreement" under which every group "knows its place" and "its school." Some examples based on unofficial and unpublished reports will illustrate this point.

The Levanim school, located in a mixed neighborhood, consisted in 1952 of 198 Orientals and 5 Ashkenazi pupils; traditionally, the Ashkenazi children of this neighborhood go to another school (Sokolov). The Levanot school had 273 Oriental and 3 Ashkenazi pupils; the Workers school, separated only by a fence from the Levanot school, consisted mainly of Ashkenazim.

Many of the Jerusalem pupils do not go to their neighborhood schools. For instance, the Oriental children of Nakhlaot walk to the Levanim school, which is located at a considerable distance. Forty per cent of the pupils studying in the school of the Beit-Hakerem suburb come by bus all the way from the city. These are mainly middle-class Ashkenazi children sent to this distant school to study with the "right" pupils and avoid association with the "wrong" ones.

Despite the lack of official statistics, the available figures reveal a high degree of *de facto* school segregation in Jerusalem.

Similar conditions prevail in other parts of the country. Only a few communities have so far established school districts, and these, too, were established without any consideration for the importance of mutual ethnic association. In the majority of communities there are no zoning regulations. The result is a high degree of segregation.

Segregation through Trends in Education

The division of the Israeli school system into publicly supported schools of three different "trends" of education—"religious," "workers," and "general"—sometimes indirectly leads to segregation. The law gives every parent the right to send his child to a school which agrees with his ideology. In practice, some parents misuse this right and send their children to the school whose population is predominantly composed of children of their ethnic group.

For instance, one of the oldest villages in the country has two elementary schools, one "general" and one "religious." The majority of the Yemenite children go to the "religious" school, while the Ashkenazi and the other Oriental pupils go to the "general" school. Although some of the non-Yemenite parents are religious, they do not send their children to the so-called religious school: in theory this school is religious, but in practice it is simply Yemenite. The ethnic factor is much stronger than the ideological. The result is ethnic segregation disguised in ideological differences.

These conditions of ethnic differentiation, falsely derived from alleged ideological differences, are especially pronounced in communities composed of new immigrants. They are manifested in various aspects of the community life, not only in the educational institutions. A participant-observer in one of these communities writes:

> The central committee of the village is officially elected according to political affiliation. In practice, however, the elections are based on a political principle which presses from without, and on an ethnic principle which presses from within. (R4:263)

In other words, while the older Israeli community is mainly divided according to, and thinks in terms of, political affiliation, many of the communities of the new immigrants are divided according to, and think in terms of, ethnic affiliation.

The Israeli general public is not aware of these and other existing forces which lead to segregation in the educational institutions. For instance, in one immigrant community there are two youth clubs. One is under the auspices of the moderate labor party (Mapai), and the other under the auspices of the left-wing party (Mapam). In the Mapai club there are almost none but Yemenite youth, and the Mapam club is composed primarily of Moroccan and Ashkenazi youth (R4:264). It would be foolish to assume that the overlapping in this community between political and ethnic affiliation is coincidental. The unpleasant truth is that the real factor which determines club affiliation, in this community as in many others, is ethnic origin.

The foregoing analysis suggests, then, that in many communities, especially those of new immigrants, (1) the enrollment in the schools representing the three educational trends coincides to some extent with ethnic differentiation, (2) the main consideration of many parents in sending their children to school is not the ideology of the school but rather its ethnic composition, and (3) many parents send their children to schools which conflict with their ideology in order to avoid association with the "wrong" pupils.

Segregation in Secondary and Higher Education

The extent of mutual association between Ashkenazi and Oriental students in the secondary schools and in the various institutions of higher education is extremely limited. In spite of the fact that the Oriental community constitutes 42 per cent of the entire Israeli population, only 5 per cent of the students enrolled in these institutions are Oriental. (C2)

The harsh truth is that these institutions do not appeal to the Oriental community. Some of the basic reasons are: high tuition, academic orientation, and a traditional lack of appreciation of secondary and higher education on the part of the Oriental community.

The majority of the Oriental students who continue their studies enter vocational high schools—the "secondary class school"—and only a small minority go to the academic high school; very few proceed to institutions of higher education.

These conditions have two major effects: (1) The secondary schools and the institutions of higher education, whose role is to educate leaders, fail to provide this training to the Oriental community, and also fail to provide the future leaders with the experience of inter-ethnic living. (2) Because of these conditions the normalization of the economic structure of the Oriental community is an increasingly remote goal.

Obstacles to the Abolition of School Segregation

The Israeli public and its leaders are for the most part unaware of the importance of mutual ethnic association in the school. Any movement or organization which would attempt to explain this principle to the public should be ready to face some resistance and obstacles.

A major obstacle is the resistance of some sectors of both the Ashkenazi community and the Oriental to the suggested changes.

Looking toward the future, one may expect that some Ashkenazi parents will resist the program of school re-zoning on some or all of the following alleged grounds: (1) It will lower the educational standards of their school and consequently lower the standard of achievement of their children. (2) Their children will learn "bad manners" and "dirty words" by associating with the lower-class Orientals. It will be especially embarrassing to the girls. (3) The lower-class Orientals are aggressive, and Ashkenazi children are not safe in associating with them. (4) There will be more danger of Ashkenazi children catching contagious diseases such as trachoma or tetter. (5) There is no objection to the inclusion of Oriental pupils, as such, in their children's school. The objection is only to the inclusion of the slum Orientals, who are "ignorant, dirty, aggressive, and not interested in learning." (6) It will be a frustrating experience for the Oriental child, with his "primitive background," to study with the "twentieth century" Ashkenazi pupil. It is preferable to provide the Oriental children with a few years of education in a separate school or class, so that they may "absorb" the modern modes of thought and behavior, and only then to transfer them to heterogeneous classes. The Oriental child has to be "prepared" to meet the Ashkenazi in order to avoid the creation of feelings of inferiority, anxiety, and frustrations. (This belief is held not only by some sectors of the Ashkenazi community, but also by a segment of the Oriental group.) (7) The idea of mutual ethnic association is most important for the integration of the nation and for the solution of the ethnic conflict, but: "Why should *our* kid carry the whole burden of social reform?"

At least one segment of the Oriental community may be expected to oppose new zoning regulations which would force mutual ethnic association in the schools. One of the few discussions of this topic can be found in an article by Israel Yeshayahu (Y5), a Yemenite leader who is devoting his life to the task of integrating the Yemenite community with the whole Israeli culture. In analyzing the self-imposed school segregation of a big sector of the Yemenite community in Tel Aviv, he emphasizes three major factors.

An example of detrimental isolationism is our insistence on separate education for Yemenite children. When we were in the exile of Yemen, we suffered because of being Jews. . . . Strangely enough, in joining our Jewish brothers in Israel we have become Yemenites and want to safeguard our Yemeniteness much more than our nationality.

There are many arguments which attempt to explain or rationalize this weakness called Yemeniteness. One argument is religion. Some of us claim that the schools of the general trend de-emphasize religion. . . . However, why don't they send their children to the schools of the religious trend, instead of segregating them in a special Yemenite school?

A second argument is that through separate schooling we wish to perpetuate some important values, such as the Yemenite pronunciation. The proponents of this view forget that the accent is only a means to an end and not an end in itself. (Y5:52)

It is relatively easy to point out the invalidity of these first two grounds claimed for self-imposed school segregation—the attempt to perpetuate a religious way of life, and the attempt to perpetuate the Yemenite culture. It is much more difficult, however, to oppose a third point: "The close association of poor Yemenite children with children who are not poor [Ashkenazim] is a source of feelings of inferiority and jealousy." (Y5:52)

This last argument is the most important factor in the reluctance of many Oriental parents, not only Yemenites, to encourage their children to associate closely with Ashkenazi pupils. It should be emphasized that living together under the common roof of the school is only the *first step* toward making this institution a major determinant in the improvement of ethnic group relations—that it cannot of itself bring improvement but may even, without the proper basis, make the situation worse. "Association with minority people on a basis which assumes their inferiority, or unworthiness, or essential difference, only stamps deeper the prevailing prejudices." (W3:69)

An analysis of the Israeli school shows that it has often unwittingly violated many of the rights of the Orientals to equality of opportunity, and intensified their inferiority feelings and the existing prejudices against them.

A movement which aims at the elimination of school segregation must look for ways of creating a school atmosphere which would be conducive to the development of healthy relations among students of diverse social classes and ethnic origins.

Before this is attempted, however, there is need for further analysis of the impact of the school on the ethnic problem, with emphasis on its influence on the Oriental pupil.

Non-attendance and Non-promotion

In 1941 Brill investigated the school attendance of the Jewish children in Jerusalem (B11). His major findings may be summarized as follows: (1) The percentage of non-attenders is 15.6: 9.6 per cent of the boys and 21.9 per cent of the girls. Of these, 2 per cent are Ashkenazi and 13.6 per cent are Orientals. (2) In addition to these "non-attenders," there are about 1,900 children who study in primitive institutions. These institutions are located in the poorer Oriental communities and are under little or no public control.

Brill cites three main reasons for the non-attendance of Jewish children in Jerusalem: (1) the apathy of the Jerusalem community, especially of the poorer Oriental Jews; (2) the peculiar economic, social, and cultural structure of the poorer Oriental communities, presenting social problems comparable to those of any semi-primitive community living within a larger and more complex Western milieu; and (3) the school organization, courses of study, and methods of teaching, which lack flexibility and provisions for individual differences and frequently result in the dull children experiencing repeated failures and leaving school to find their personal successes in the streets.

Similar conclusions were reached by Bachi in his study, *The Hebrew Pupil in Jerusalem.* (B2)

A recent study on this topic reached more comprehensive and definite conclusions:

1) In contradistinction to the Ashkenazim, the Oriental pupil finds schooling much more difficult. 56% of the Orientals, in comparison to 23% of the Ashkenazim, are not promoted somewhere along the educational ladder. 2) The major cause for the small number of Oriental pupils in the eighth grade is early non-promotion, which results in despair and early school leaving. 59% of the Orientals remain in school for the full course of eight years, but only 46% reach the eighth grade. 3) The overwhelming majority of school mortality cases are those who were not promoted once or twice.

In conclusion: The major cause for the school mortality is failure in school, as manifested in non-promotion. (O1:23)

The above investigations, all of them made before 1948, show that school mortality has been one of the most acute problems of the Israeli school. It was hoped that the Compulsory Elementary Education Law, enacted in 1949, would solve the drop-out problem and result in many more elementary school graduates. This hope, however, proved to be unsound.

A recent study by Enoch (E13) shows that the city has many children who fail to graduate from elementary school. The reason is not so much failure to attend school for a full eight years as non-promotion. The yearly rate of non-promotion is 10 per cent. In other words, out of 100 children who enter the first grade, only 45 graduate from the elementary school, eight years later.

An analysis of these figures reveals that it is mainly with respect to the Oriental child that non-promotion is a problem. In Tel Aviv the average Ashkenazi pupil completes the elementary school, while the average Oriental fails once or twice to be promoted and consequently does not graduate.

Enoch also found a high correlation among economic conditions, Oriental origin, and non-promotion. Only 43 per cent of the school population is Oriental; however, approximately 66 per cent of the school failures come from this group. They compose 50 per cent of first graders, but only 23 per cent of the pupils in the eighth grade.

The conclusion of Enoch's investigation is:

> The Compulsory Education Law will succeed in forcing parents to leave their children in the school until they reach the age of fourteen; however it will hardly increase the number of elementary school graduates or the level of education of the group who needs it most. The goal of elementary education for every Israeli child will never be attained without the eradication of the curse of non-promotion. (E13:39)

The non-promotion policy in the school is very detrimental to the mental health and social development of the Oriental community and is one of the major stumbling blocks on the road to social integration.

A major approach to the integration of the two ethnic groups is raising the socio-economic standard of living of the Oriental community. In our culture, formal education is a prerequisite to social advancement; consequently, a non-promotion policy makes the school an instrument for creating the very inequalities it was designed to prevent and cure. Instead of becoming the means for eliminating ethnic and class distinctions, the school often establishes them more firmly by closing the gates of further education and social advancement to the majority of the Oriental children. The non-promotion policy results in the creation of two groups—a group of school graduates, mainly Ashkenazim, for whom the specialized occupations are opened, and another group, the "repeaters," who lack education and can become only "hewers of wood and drawers of water."

Non-promotion is prevalent especially among the Orientals in the first grade. Brill (B11) found that 25 per cent of the Orientals in comparison to 7.3 per cent of the Ashkenazim were retarded in the first grade. The recent findings of Enoch (E13) present a much darker picture. They show that the ratio of retardation in the first grade is seven Orientals to one Ashkenazi. In percentage: Orientals, 22.2; Ashkenazim, 3.2.

Already in the first grade the non-promoted pupil develops a negative attitude toward the school, the teacher, and the educational and spiritual values represented by this institution. The experience of failure constitutes a source of insecurity, emotional instability, and lack of interest in school activities. These children often become discipline problems and sometimes even juvenile delinquents.

> The non-promoted pupils are hurt psychologically and feel inferior to their peers. They become negative forces full of resentment and envy. At present, they contribute the largest number of juvenile delinquents, and in the future they will probably be a burden on the welfare agencies. (B8:13)

Remembering that the non-promoted child is mainly of Oriental origin, and that the school teachers are mainly Ashkenazim, we may hypothesize that some Oriental pupils conceive of their school failure as another manifestation of the way in which the dominant Ashkenazi majority treats the Oriental minority. It then becomes "legitimate" to react to such treatment in various forms of antisocial behavior.

The non-promotion policy is detrimental not only to the Oriental child but also to his parents and his community. The parent is faced with the bitter reality that his hope of helping his child advance through schooling cannot be achieved. The child's failure only intensifies the parent's own sense of failure in being on the "wrong side of the tracks." The parents' unfulfilled hopes lead to friction between the two generations.

Efforts to change the motivational pattern of the lower-class Orientals and to convince them that schooling is a major avenue for self-improvement and social mobility are nullified by the fact that so many of their children fail as early as in the first grade, and that the majority of their sons and daughters do not succeed in graduating from elementary school.

The land of Israel is poor in natural resources. The country's major resource is the people. A satisfactory standard of living will be achieved only if these people are motivated to improve their life through the development of their social and technical skills.

The present policy of non-promotion dooms a great sector of the Israeli population to a status of semi-illiteracy, and generates in it an apathetic and even negative attitude toward education and self-improvement. Consequently this policy is detrimental to the future growth, security, and welfare of the country and its inhabitants.

Failure and Low Status of the Oriental Pupil

The non-promoted pupils are the most extreme manifestation of failure in the school. They are representatives of a much bigger group of students for whom life in school means boredom, tension, hardship, punishment, low achievement, feelings of inferiority and jealousy, and waste of time. This bigger group is mainly composed of Oriental pupils. One may summarize the status of the average Oriental pupil by saying: he is the problem child of the school.

The school will never become a major determinant in the improvement of ethnic relations unless the causes underlying these conditions are diagnosed and remedied.

The major factors in the status of the Oriental pupil will be analyzed under the following three headings: (1) intelligence; (2) lower-class belongingness; and (3) the curriculum.

INTELLIGENCE

Low intelligence is considered by many Israeli educators a major cause of the failure of the Oriental pupil.

Bakaliar (B4) compared the verbal intelligence of Yemenite with that of non-Yemenite graduates of elementary schools in Tel Aviv. She found that the median of the first group was 29 per cent lower than the median of the latter. On a non-verbal intelligence test the median of the Yemenite boys was 10 per cent lower than the median of the non-Yemenite boys, and the median of the Yemenite girls was 25 per cent lower than the median of the non-Yemenite girls. A battery of motor aptitude tests showed that the median of the Yemenite boys was one per cent lower than the median of the non-Yemenite ones. In interpreting the results, Bakaliar says:

> The verbal intelligence tests are based on knowledge of the language, which is a product of the education, amount of reading, and socio-economic level of the testees. . . . The non-verbal and aptitude tests are much less influenced by the specific environment and consequently the differences between the two groups on these tests are very slight. (B4:322)

Comparing the intelligence of Ashkenazi pupils with various groups of Oriental pupils, Oestreicher (O3) found that: (1) The Oriental groups are considerably lower than the Ashkenazi on verbal tests, but not much lower on arithmetic tests. The poor socio-economic conditions are more positively related to ability in abstract linguistic reasoning than to arithmetic ability. (2) When the two ethnic groups are equated for socio-economic background the differences on the tests are not statistically significant. In other words, the differences existing between the two groups are related to their socio-economic background rather than to their ethnic origin.

Many teachers maintain that even when the general intelligence of the Oriental pupil is satisfactory, he still lacks the power of abstract reasoning which is required for mastery of the subject matter.

Ortar attempted to investigate this problem in a study on "Differences in the Structure of Intelligence—A Comparative Analysis of Ethnic Sub-Groups." Comparing three groups of pupils—Ashkenazim, old-timer Orientals, and newcomer Orientals—she concludes that:

1) Differences in socio-economic and cultural environments resulted in differences in intelligence among the various Israeli ethnic groups.
2) Equated for the general level of intelligence, the three groups show qualitative differences in the structure of their intelligence.
3) Under the influence of the Israeli environment the qualitative differences in intelligence tend to become smaller. Equated for the general level of intelligence, only the newly arrived Orientals, and not the old-timers, are lower than the Ashkenazim in abstract reasoning. (O6:122)

Evidence that the Israeli environment raises the level of intelligence of the Orientals is pointed out in another study. Comparing a segregated and a non-segregated group of Yemenite pupils, Bakaliar found that the second showed higher results on non-verbal intelligence tests. "It is possible that when the Yemenite pupils are distributed over various schools their general level of intelligence tends to rise." (B3:159)

Students of ethnic problems in other countries have reached similar conclusions concerning environmental influences on less privileged groups. (K4)

As the environment of the different ethnic groups becomes more similar, differences in test scores are reduced. The environment of the veteran Oriental is closer to that of the Ashkenazim than the environment of the newcomer Oriental. This difference is responsible for their improved scores. In spite of these improvements, the goal of equality is still remote.

Upon reading these studies and hearing the Israeli teacher complain about the low mentality of the Oriental child, the impression is received that low intelligence is the major factor in the difficulties and the low status of this ethnic group in the school. A critical analysis of the intelligence factor, however, reveals that this conclusion is only partly justified.

Investigating the impact of social class membership on adolescents in Elmtown, Hollingshead attempted to answer the following question: Is academic failure in the lower class linked with lack of intellectual capacity? He found that

> Although intelligence was associated significantly with class position, the degree of association was not high enough to account for the concentration of failures in the lower class. Neither was it great enough to attribute the high grades in the upper classes to the intellectual capacity of this prestige level. Behind the stark figures of grades received in courses and scores made on intelligence tests lies the Elmtown social system. (H6:175)

Although intelligence is positively correlated with school marks, it does not fully account for the higher percentage of academic failures among the Oriental pupils. The Orientals encounter more failure in the school than the non-Oriental pupils who are below average in intelligence. One must look for other factors, more important than intelligence, to understand this school failure. At the root of the failure of the Oriental child on the intelligence test and in the school may well be the Israeli social system.

Another important question is: Can the present intelligence tests be used to predict educability—the potentiality for education existing in an individual or in a group?

> From the standpoint of the practical work of the schools, the problem of educability can take one of two forms—
> a) Given our present schools, with the ends which they accept and the means which they provide, what measurable characteristics of persons can be used to predict the extent to which these persons will do successful work in the schools?
> b) What measurable characteristics of persons can be identified that reveal abilities which can be developed into socially or personally valuable behavior if school programs are planned and administered to capitalize on these activities? (T11:39)

The first formulation of the problem accepts the schools as they are; the second formulation, however, looks for a new type of school.

In the present school, the major predictive measure of pupil educability, or academic success as indicated by a teacher's marks, is the intelligence test. It is known that, of all the kinds of pupil behavior measured by intelligence tests, the use of words is most closely related to school progress. The mean correlation between verbal intelligence and school grades is generally considered to be 0.50, a figure reached by no other type of intelligence test. Similar results were obtained in Israel. (S4:167–8)

Intelligence tests are culturally loaded in favor of middle-class children. The experiences of middle-class children are highly correlated with the content of these tests. Part of the content is unfamiliar to most lower-class children. (D3, E2)

The so-called "general intelligence tests" fail to give an indication of a variety of abilities that could be developed if the aims and experiences of the school were broadened. These tests have been validated in terms of school marks. Items have been discarded which did not show high correlation with the school marks of subjects who answered the question correctly. These good students were mainly middle-class students. This procedure has greatly increased test validity, at the cost of making it more difficult for lower-class children, whatever their native endowments, to make high scores. The experiences and special abilities typical for their class have not entered into these school intelligence tests. But as Tyler says,

Youngsters who do not show up well on intelligence tests do possess abilities that indicate some skill in solving practical problems and that suggest potentialities for further education if the schools had broad enough goals to utilize talents of these kinds. (T11:43)

The Israeli educator, in attempting to construct intelligence tests, also committed the mistake of making them culturally loaded and class biased. An examination of a recent study (S4) will substantiate this claim. Comparing the mental development of Oriental and Ashkenazi children, Shur constructed tests of general information, vocabulary, and understanding of pictures. She says:

> In looking for test items we were helped by the course of study and readers of the first grade. We included in the general information test, problems needed in the understanding of the subject matter taught in the first grade. In measuring the child's vocabulary we attempted to see his understanding of the terminology in the primary reader. We attempted to measure his understanding of the pictures which illustrate the primary readers. (S4:47)

No wonder that success on these tests highly correlates with success in the first grade. Many of the test items were better answered by the Ashkenazi pupil not because of his richer personal experiences, but because these items are symbols emphasized in the Ashkenazi home, the primary reader, and the classroom. For instance, to an item dealing with the signs of the morning, the children reacted by describing the rising of the sun or the cry of the rooster. (S4:58) They had learned this type of answer through vicarious rather than through firsthand experiences. The Oriental children do not have such vicarious experiences because their preschool environment does not prepare them for the academic culture of the school. The results are lower scores on the tests and lower grades at school.

A further examination of the above tests shows that the Oriental group scored higher on a few items (for instance, "What does mother do when the baby cries?" or "What is the price of ice-cream?"). The Oriental child scored higher on these items because they tapped areas in which he had a greater firsthand experience than the Ashkenazi child.

We may postulate that a test on which the Orientals would score higher than the Ashkenazim could be constructed. Unfortunately, no such test has ever been compiled. To the class-biased test constructors, "information" has always meant the information held by the Ashkenazi group.

The area of arithmetic furnishes support for the claim that a test might be class biased and culturally loaded. A comparison of Oriental and Ashkenazi children in arithmetic shows only slight differences in favor of the latter. (O1) In interpreting these results, some writers have maintained that arithmetic is an area not influenced by the child's specific environment. (S4:167) This is highly questionable. Both cultures stimulate the child's growth in arithmetic—the Ashkenazi culture through deliberate training, the Oriental culture through firsthand and vicarious experiences. Moreover, arithmetic is an area where both the testing and the school program succeeded to some extent in capitalizing on the talents and on the experiences of the two cultures. Consequently, arithmetic tests show only slight differences between the two.

The limited and class-biased concept of intelligence has a negative effect on attempts to improve the curriculum and adapt it to the needs of the various ethnic groups. The results of these tests enhance the notion that the Oriental group has a low potential of educability. Teachers often conclude that the only possible "remedy" is an increase of activities based on the middle-class culture and verbal training. But this only intensifies the very problem it tries to solve and results in low morale among teachers and pupils.

Speaking about the urgent need to improve the intelligence tests, Tyler calls for an attack on two fronts:

a) On the identification and measurement of abilities which indicate talents that can be developed by educational means.
b) On experimentation with learnings so that we may know how to capitalize on the talents that are thus identified. (T11:46)

The two approaches are interrelated. Only the first one, however, is under discussion in this section. The construction of measures of these more varied educability potentials will help the educator in capitalizing on a wide range of abilities not now utilized by the typical Israeli school.

Israel, faced with the problem of increasing productiveness, must aim to discover many kinds of talents in its pupils and to find ways to develop them. To attain this goal, we must have a method or an instrument for measuring the real innate intelligence of the various people, no matter how poor their environment has been. Developing these new tests is one of the greatest contributions measurement experts can make to the growth of the nation and to the solution of the ethnic group problem.

THE LOWER-CLASS CHILD IN A MIDDLE-CLASS SCHOOL

Behind the failure and lower status of the Oriental pupil lies the Israeli social system. Taking non-promotion as an indicator of failure, and room density in the home as a clue to socio-economic conditions, a study of the Tel Aviv school system shows that they are closely related (E13:46):

Room Density	Average Non-promotion
2.1–2.7	4.8%
2.8–3.6	9.4%
3.7–6.2	17.1%

A social class to some extent determines the goals, motivations, attitudes, experiences, and behavior of its members. To understand the total behavior of a child, one must include a consideration of his social class position and the cultural expectation of his group.

The fact that the division of the Israeli population into two ethnic groups largely coincides with a division into a middle and a lower class has already been discussed, in Chapter IV. The following discussion is concerned with (1) the different expectations which these two classes hold toward their children, and (2) a comparison between these expectations and the expectations of the school.

Class Expectations. There are hardly any studies on class patterns in Israel. The analysis must be limited mainly to the observations of the writer and based on the ten categories developed by the Kluckhohns (K5) in their study of class patterns in America.

1. The middle-class Ashkenazi child is encouraged to save money and to take care of his possessions. This expectation is part of a belief in the importance and practicability of planning ahead. The lower-class Oriental child is allowed to spend money as he wishes, when he has the money. The pattern of saving and planning is not reinforced by successful results in this culture.

2. For the Ashkenazi child sexual interests and talk are taboo. The same taboos exist with regard to the Oriental child; however, he hears much more talk about sexual activities and sometimes even observes them.

3. The Ashkenazi culture emphasizes such matters as cleanliness, regular bowel movement at an early age, table manners, greeting customs, keeping rooms in order, and so forth. The Oriental culture emphasizes these things to a lesser extent, and some of its sectors even neglect them.

4. Aggression and temper of middle-class children are controlled and channelized into verbal expression. In the lower class there is less restriction on expression of overt aggression, and in some sectors fighting is encouraged by the gang.

5. The middle-class Ashkenazi child is culturally motivated to suffer privations and renounce gratifications in order to achieve success later. The drive for achievement is less valued among the Orientals, and their level of aspiration is much lower. A study of vocational interests of urban youth (M4) shows that twice as many Ashkenazi as Orientals prefer to be professional workers. The fact that the Oriental sample in the study is composed of elementary school graduates and therefore represents a selected group suggests that the real differences in vocational interests of the whole population are much greater. Some sectors of the Oriental Jewry are characterized by passivity and almost no emphasis on achievement and social climbing.

6. The middle-class child is expected to comply with the regulations and laws of society and to conform to the rules of the school and other groups and institutions. In some sectors of the lower class, a child is taught to fear, rather than to respect, authority. In these sectors an attitude of "do it and try not to get caught" is prevalent.

7. The Ashkenazi child is expected to associate only with playmates who are acceptable to his parents. The peer relations are supervised and criticized. Parents encourage friendship by inviting children to the home. In the Oriental group a boy is free to select his friends with little or no interference by his parents. A girl growing up is much more supervised, but in many cases with little success.

8. The Ashkenazi child is encouraged to have hobbies, to join out-of-school activities such as music courses or the Scouts. Parents take children on trips and call their attention to what is noteworthy in the surrounding scene. Movie visits are limited and supervised. These deliberate encouragements, stimulations, and restrictions do not exist in many sectors of the Oriental community.

9. Middle-class children (especially boys) are expected to do very

little around the household or in helping the father on his job. Lower-class children are expected to take care of younger siblings, share in the household responsibilities, and often help the father on his job. In some Oriental sectors the child is expected to quit school at an early age and get a job. A few years ago the employment of young Oriental girls (aged ten to thirteen) as housemaids was common. (P5) The emphasis in getting a job is not on its training aspect but rather on the desire to get the maximum immediate remuneration, with almost no consideration of the future. (F7)

10. Among the Ashkenazim, the traditional admiration of those learned in the Torah, the aspirations that Israel should become the "spiritual center" for the Diaspora, the belief that only a high level of specialization can solve the socio-economic problems of the country, and the emphasis on individual achievement and success, have combined together into a faith in education as the major channel for the fulfillment of national and personal goals.

Ashkenazi parents expect their children to do well in school. Interest and anxiety about school success is inculcated through reward and punishment. Good grades and report cards are rewarded by praise or gifts. The yearly graduation day is celebrated by all who are promoted. When the child reports any behavior difficulties in the school, the parents support the teacher rather than their own child. Parents (especially the mother) try to meet the teacher, and many of them are ready to support the school activities (especially in the first grade).

They are also willing to make great economic sacrifices in order to send their child to high school. The aspiration of the parents is that their children (especially their daughters) will study in an academic high school. The vocational high school is only a second choice. (E12) In recent years, moreover, emphasis on college education has greatly increased. (R6)

Many lower-class Orientals take no daily interest in the education of their children. Shur (S4) has found that on entering school the Oriental pupils have more limited information, not because of lack of first-hand experiences, but because of the failure of the adults to increase the general knowledge of their children by interpreting the phenomena which surround them.

A large segment of these people have little appreciation for the work of the school or for the benefits their children might derive from it.

The continuous experience of failure to advance socially through schooling reinforces their indifference to education. Some poor sectors consider schooling a needless drain on the family budget and think that
boys and girls, especially girls, ought to be working. (F7, R4)

This apathetic or sometimes even negative attitude toward the
school is enhanced by their contact with the school personnel—teachers
and administrators. They know that an invitation to or a note from the
school means that their child has done something wrong. A visit of a
school representative to their home is resented because it means criticism and being told "how to do it better." (S4)

Similar conclusions about the contact between the school and the
lower class in America were reached in Hollingshead's study of *Elmtown's Youth*. (H6) A statistical analysis of teacher-parent conferences shows that while some parents from all social classes were counseled, almost all discipline problems involved lower-class parents. On
the other hand, lower-class parents were counseled less than the middle-
class parents in respect to school work and grades, although the
lower-class children made the poorest marks.

These facts partly explain the reluctance of lower-class parents to
come to the school to visit or to confer about their children. They do
not feel comfortable in the school setting.

School Expectations. The above analysis shows that the lower-class
Oriental culture and the middle-class Ashkenazi culture teach their
children patterns of behavior which differ in basic respects. The school,
however, does not pay much attention to these basic differences. It tends
to support middle-class and to disapprove of lower-class values.

A look at a typical report card may give some insight into the behavior the school expects from pupils. In addition to a general statement about success or failure in the various subjects, the pupil is graded
according to the following traits: conduct, orderliness, cleanliness, and
industriousness. In other words, the school expects children to be neat
and clean, to refrain from fighting and using bad language, to care for
property and use materials wisely, to be prompt in attendance, to comply
with the teacher's regulations, to concentrate on their work and make
every effort to "achieve."

These traits of behavior are consistent with the expectations which
middle-class parents have for their children. The home and the school

reinforce each other. For the lower-class Oriental child, however, the school expectations with regard to behavior are quite at variance with his parents'. The teacher may teach his group that it is not nice to curse, whereas the child from the slums knows that many of his friends curse habitually. The teacher may punish, for being aggressive, children who are expected at home to fight for their rights.

Many of the primary grade teachers have a daily check-up of cleanliness, accompanied by singing about cleanliness, rewarding of the clean children, and disapproving of the dirty ones. (S4) This is done without any consideration of the conflicts it generates in a child who comes from a home which does not emphasize cleanliness to the same extent.

One reason for the heavy emphasis placed on middle-class values is the fact that the school personnel is composed of an overwhelming majority of Ashkenazi teachers and a very small minority of Oriental teachers. Most of the latter are middle-class Sephardim.

In order for a child to learn from a socializing agent, he must be rewarded and accepted by him. However, the acceptance which Oriental children need in order to learn is sometimes denied to them. Teachers often find it difficult really to accept pupils whose cultural background is very different from their own.

In the book *The Father of the Man,* (D1) two American scholars present some case studies which illustrate this conflict in values between the lower class and the school expectations. The Israeli literature, scientific and general, has yet to explore this area.

The educator may question the assumption that patterns and values of the middle-class home, which are reinforced by the middle-class school, are the most desirable and should be inculcated in children.

> Punctuality, neatness, docility and work mindedness are all well and good; but missing are expectations that might be considered more fundamental such as the development of intellectual curiosity, confidence in one's self, ability to get along with other children, respect for all individuals regardless of ethnic group or social class, developing insights into one's self and others, training into use of scientific method for solving problems, development of moral courage and moral integrity. (A2:93)

An important factor, then, in the failure and low status of the lower-class Oriental pupil is the fact that he brings with him to school patterns of behavior which are at variance with the school expectations.

In contrast to the middle-class Ashkenazi child, he does not bring with him to school a great faith in the importance of education and he is not motivated by his parents and his culture to renounce and to postpone gratifications in order to achieve academic or professional goals.

Only a high level of aspiration to improve oneself, and strong motivation to achieve and conform, can help a pupil to succeed in the present academically loaded curriculum. An analysis of the school curriculum may reveal the third basic cause, and it may be the most important one, for the failure of the Oriental pupil.

THE CURRICULUM

Here is a scene for the pen of a satirist. Place: an Israeli high school. Setting: an era marked by unrest and deprivation, problems of cultural and economic rehabilitation of half a million refugees, ethnic tension, political intrigues. . . . And what are the children in the school in this era learning? They learn that the square of the sum of two numbers equals the sum of their squares plus twice their product; they memorize the names of Jacob's twelve sons, and the details of the war between Athens and Sparta.

That the non-functionality of the school curriculum is responsible for the failure of the Oriental pupil has already been argued by Brill. "The course of study of the Israeli schools . . . was compiled thirty years ago by Ashkenazi teachers and was adapted to the abilities and characteristics of the Ashkenazi child. . . . No wonder that the Oriental child fails in such a school." (B10:14)

It is questionable whether this curriculum meets the needs of any child; it is adapted neither to the needs of the Orientals nor to the needs of the Ashkenazim. The average Ashkenazi pupil, however, because of home pressure and expectations, is able to "survive" the curriculum, while the average Oriental pupil fails. The school is not doing a satisfactory job of educating the Ashkenazi child and is especially poor in educating the Oriental.

In support of these claims, the curriculum will be examined from the points of view of (1) its content and structure, (2) its method of presentation, and (3) its contribution to the building of democratic behavior.

Content and Structure. A primary principle of the Israeli school curriculum is that a certain body of knowledge is essential for all children —a body of knowledge which has been valued for a long time and is handed down on authority, largely intact, from generation to generation. The curriculum is composed of the study of the "essentials" of Jewish and world culture. Over the years, subject after subject has been added, under pressure of specialists and the public, to this curriculum of "essentials."

The content of the various fields was initially selected on the basis of the traditional arrangement of the subjects, with relatively little regard for their relation to the child's experiences. The result is a school curriculum loaded with a great body of knowledge which is largely meaningless to many students.

The central idea behind the subject-matter basis of curriculum organization is that each subject possesses a certain logic and organization of its own. The principal means to education is systematic study of the various subjects. The students learn to recognize and reproduce symbols which have little or no meaning for them, and to recite textbook definitions without real understanding.

A further indictment of the subject curriculum may be made on the grounds of its compartmentalized and fragmentary nature. It is obvious that in meeting usual life situations a combination of various subjects is nearly always involved. The problems facing people are not divided according to language, history, and arithmetic. In attempting to cope with life situations, the individual has to draw together information from various subject fields. The subject curriculum operates in the opposite direction. It focuses on the subject and utilizes life situations only for illustration, instead of making life problems the center of the curriculum.

Another objection to the subject curriculum in Israeli schools is that it ignores current and persistent social problems; it is mainly an exposition of what has been done in the past. The student learns more about the Maccabees than about labor-management relations, more about political problems at the time of Jeremiah than about present political systems, more about the anatomy of a flower than about health provisions in the country. There is little concern for ethnic group problems and social class differences. There is no attempt to study the real problems of the family, no attempt to help children express their anxieties and feelings and get insight into the dynamics of their behavior and the behavior of others. In short, the emphasis is on the traditions of the past and not on the problems of the present or the planning of the future.

The subject curriculum ignores the interests of the learner. The learnings most conducive to growth are those involving problems that the learner is facing and is interested in solving. The present curriculum appeals only to those students who are either interested in academic achievements or hoping to gain social approval through good grades.

Faced with this great obstacle—the failure of the subject curriculum to arouse intrinsic motivation in the pupil—the school elaborated a system of extrinsic motivations, such as marks, promotions, and the teacher's "bag of tricks." An analysis of these techniques of motivation may reveal that they are much more harmful than the content and the structure of the subject curriculum itself.

Method of Presentation. The major emphasis in teaching methods is placed upon techniques of explanation. Two camps are created in the classroom. Facing the class stands an active and dynamic teacher who attempts to be interesting and to prove to the pupils that he is an authority on the subject. The teacher lectures, demonstrates, asks questions, plans, and acts. Facing the teacher, the students sit silently and passively. Their task is to digest the information which is poured into them.

The procedure which has had the largest effect upon the Israeli school, and particularly on the elementary school, is the Herbartian lesson plan. It is composed of five formal steps: (1) preparation, (2) presentation, (3) comparison and abstractions, (4) generalization, and (5) application. According to this lesson plan, the teacher reveals to his "followers" at any given time not more than the immediate next step of his plan. At the end of the lesson the "pupil's objective" is achieved. Then the class is supposed to wait passively for the next session, when the teacher is going to present a new objective which no one of the pupils had any part in formulating. If the teacher forgets to make an assignment, the student is free and has no responsibility to pursue further learning.

Working with student teachers, the writer found that in performing demonstration lessons they concealed the next topic from their pupils and hid the new posters, records, and other materials. The student teacher wanted to arouse class interest by surprising and fascinating the pupils with the richness of the materials which he prepared and preplanned.

It is not difficult to recognize in this description the attributes of authoritarian leadership. It is the teacher who determines the goal and plans the policy of the group; it is the leader's "field of power" which keeps the pupils going.

The pupils have the feeling that the lesson is the teacher's business and not their own. Their protest is expressed in various forms—from non-attention to organized disturbances.

In order to make students learn what they would not learn of their own accord, the teacher devises not only a fascinating art of presenting the subject but also a system of extrinsic motivation. Rewards and punishments are continually used in the classroom to make some ways of behaving pleasurable and other ways painful. Rewards are not limited to marks, promotions, or stars; nor is punishment limited to non-promotion or expulsion from the group. The nod of approval, the reassuring smile, the frown, and criticism are subtle ways in which the teacher rewards or punishes a particular act of behavior.

Observing a teacher at work, one finds that the signs of approval and disapproval are not distributed equally among all the pupils. Already in the first grade the class is sorted into two groups: the approved and the disapproved. The approved pupils are those who obey the teacher's requests for attention, follow her directions, do neat, clean work, keep obviously busy, and finish their work on time. The disapproved pupils are those who for various reasons cannot keep up with the others and cannot measure up to the same standards.

Those who belong to the disapproved group introject the teacher's evaluations of them. They lose their security and initiative and stop investing effort in mastering the subject matter. They develop a defeatist approach toward the school and the teacher, which in turn brings about more disapproval from the teacher, and consequently more rebellion toward the educating agent. A vicious circle is created. More future citizens lose the opportunity for better education and thus lose their chances to raise their socio-economic standard of living.

In order to arouse interest and keep the discussion going, the teacher bombards the class with questions. It is not a discussion where everyone contributes from his experiences, hopes, and uncertainties. It is an aggressive search for the correct answer which only a few pupils can provide immediately.

The teacher, being interested in a "good discussion," tends to prefer those who can produce the right answer and tends to ignore the other students. A discussion pattern is established where the class is divided into an active group, which has something to contribute, and a passive group, which is considered by the teacher and by itself as worthless. It is this type of destructive education that Kelley criticizes:

> When we allow people to think they have nothing to contribute, or even make them think so, we are denying the evidence all around us. If we were going on a picnic, or building a boat, or making a garden, we would expect . . . that every one would be able to contribute in some way. It is only in school that we seem to think that only the leader or a few of the "more able" are the only ones who can produce. (K2:5)

The foregoing discussion pointed out that the content and organization of the subject curriculum, the techniques of presentation, and their reliance on extrinsic motivation result in polarization of the classroom into a "successful" and a "failing" group. The first group is composed mainly of Ashkenazim. They are motivated by their home expectations to overcome all these hurdles and are helped in the preparation of the daily homework. (S4) The "failing group" is composed mainly of Orientals who do not have such stimulation and assistance.

Building Democratic Behavior. The present curriculum can be further criticized in the light of the needs and values of a democratic society.

Schools can build democratic behavior only as they become a democracy operating through the beliefs and practices which are basic to democratic living. The present Israeli school does not operate on such principles and fails to promote democratic values.

The level of cooperation in the school is very low. The student works *for* the teacher rather than *with* the teacher, and is often competing with his peers. The pupil is supposed to work by himself at a desk as though he were not surrounded by others. The "well-behaved child" is the pupil who during the lesson pays least attention to his friends and does not help them or receive help from them.

The system of reward and punishment, various competitive games, and especially the marking system generate an atmosphere of competition and enhance the need to work alone, since exchanging ideas and sharing materials might help the competitor.

> By working alone to one's own advantage and to the detriment of others the walls of isolation between people are built higher and stronger.

These walls work directly against the improvement of human relations so essential to living in our complex society. (K2:7)

These "walls of isolation" are especially high and strong between students who belong to different ethnic groups and social classes.

Every child has a need for security. He wants to establish reciprocal relations with his peers. He wants to feel that he is an accepted and valued member of the group. This is the way the child builds his self-esteem, security, and social competence.

The Oriental child finds it more difficult than the Ashkenazi child does to achieve these goals in the classroom. Both he and the Ashkenazi pupil are aware that he is "different" and is not well equipped to rate high in academic competition. He has little opportunity to establish close preschool or out-of-school relations with the Ashkenazi pupils, and the competitive and individualistic atmosphere makes it difficult to establish these relations in the school. A curriculum based on the principle of cooperation may diminish the ethnic barrier.

When people cooperate, they are learning about each other, depending upon each other, and developing confidence in each other. The process throws people into situations where it is possible for better human relations to emerge. It is an attack upon the barriers that separate people and tend to make them suspicious of each other. (K2:6)

Children need group experience if they are to learn to work together in the school and outside of school. In this atmosphere of "give and take," bonds of friendship and group solidarity develop. Only under these conditions is there a hope that the underprivileged Oriental will achieve a sense of belongingness, importance, and group acceptance.

Another characteristic of the Israeli school system which is a deterrent to the development of group life is the lack of extracurricular activities such as school committees and clubs. Problem-solving activities, neglected by the subject curriculum, are the basis for operation in many such committees and clubs. Editing a school paper, working on a school government committee, or planning a game provides excellent opportunities for the development of mature thinking, responsibility, cooperativeness, and self-directiveness.

While the typical classroom activities such as discussion, questions and answers, written exercises, and oral reports favor the individual who is capable of verbal learning, the clubs can provide a field of expression and satisfaction for students who have non-academic talents. Painting, modeling, cartooning, constructing, and designing are seldom used in the present subject curriculum, but are very well suited to these school organizations.

Work with Oriental children in camps, playgrounds, and schools shows that they gain a sense of achievement and satisfaction through such non-academic activities. (E6, N1) In other words, the relative lack of extracurricular activities restricts the school's provisions for the non-academic child, and hampers the development of "school spirit" and democratic behavior.

It would be unfair to claim that the Israeli school does not aim at the development of democratic ideals and behavior. However, instead of teaching them through experiences and practices, the school sticks mainly to the old method of exhortation. The rationale for this naive method is that the pupil will retain in memory the ideas given in the assigned lesson or story about friendliness, consideration, and honesty and will use these ideas when the appropriate time shall come. It is evident, however, that what this approach achieves at best is to teach ideas *about* democratic behavior.

The whole problem of educating for pioneering Zionism and civic-mindedness, especially as related to the Oriental problem, should be re-examined in the light of this criticism.

The Israeli school sees as one of its functions education for rural living. The stories in the readers, the arithmetic problems, and especially the songs and the celebrations are centered around aspects of rural living. On every occasion the teacher preaches to the students that the fulfillment of Zionism means ploughing of the land. Despite these tremendous efforts, the number of school graduates who leave the city to live in rural areas is very small. (E12) These efforts are not successful, partly because educators fail to see that exhortation has little effect on conduct.

Pioneering Zionism should be taught mainly through experiences. The youth movement succeeds to some extent in providing its members, mainly Ashkenazi, with opportunities to experience rural living. The Oriental youth, however, lacks this chance. No wonder that so few urban Orientals are ready to choose agriculture as a way of living. The school is partly responsible for these results.

The same can be said about civic education. The problems of reconstruction and rehabilitation confronting every community, old and new, are enormous. The present method of preparing youth to face these problems—learning stories about young people in various lands who helped their community, or hearing speeches about civic-mindedness and responsibility—will result only in the acquisition of the ability to repeat these phrases and slogans.

Ashkenazi young people learn some civic-mindedness through identification with the various activities, mainly philanthropic, which their families are engaged in, through the youth movement, and through a few limited school activities. The Oriental youth, however, lives in a disintegrated community which, in contradistinction to the Ashkenazi community, lacks a strong tradition of civic-mindedness. The school remains the major channel through which the Oriental child can develop civic-mindedness. The exhortation approach of the school to civic education is not very helpful in this respect. It does not provide the Orientals with the best opportunities to learn how to help their fellow citizens and themselves.

The school should look for ways and means of teaching desirable civic attitudes and skills through experiences. Only if the student will practice serving his community during his school years (R5) is there hope that he will continue to do it in adulthood.

"Trends" and the Ethnic Problem

The Israeli school system is divided into networks of schools of four "trends" ("general," "workers," and two branches of "religious") each enjoying the same measure of governmental support. The different school networks reflect genuine differences among the elements of the Israeli population in social attitudes and values. (R3) The proponents of each view it as a practical instrument for the realization of their ideals. The opponents of the trends deplore their divisive character, arguing that the energies of the country should be directed toward the creation of a harmonious and integrated nation. The public in general and educators in particular are fully aware of this problem. They are not fully aware, however, of the impact of the "trend" system on the ethnic problem. Three consequences of this system will be analyzed here.

ETHNIC SEGREGATION

We have seen that in many communities, primarily those of new immigrants, the division into trends coincides with ethnic differentiation. When the boards of education awaken to the need of establishing school zones based on mutual ethnic association, the division into trends will constitute a major deterrent to this plan. The boards of the various trends will be hesitant to support such a movement for fear it may decrease the enrollment in their trend, by arousing hostility of those who are reluctant to send their children to mixed schools. The trends enable ethnic segregation under the disguise of ideological differences. Consequently they jeopardize any future attempt to encourage ethnic association through the enacting of new zoning regulations.

DEMORALIZING COMPETITION

The "war among trends" in the Israeli school system—begun in 1948, with the beginning of the mass immigrations—is one of the saddest episodes in the life of the new State. It is most destructive to the integration of the various ethnic groups and to the rehabilitation of the new immigrants. Faced with the need to double the school enrollment, the various political parties and the powerful Workers' Union started a wild competition to increase the enrollment of their affiliated trends, using threats and various pressures to achieve their objectives, assuming that the end justified the means. (L2) The demoralizing effect of this conflict can be seen in the situation described by an Oriental immigrant:

> Yesterday they came and said that we had to register at school. Today others came and said that it is a bad school and that we have to go to another school. So we registered again. Then they began to shout. The teachers ran after the children and each one pulled them to his school. These are not teachers—this is not a school. These are like wild people. The children will never learn anything under these conditions. (E4:149)

These notorious conditions resulted in a continuous flow of students from one trend to another, in truancy, in serious discipline problems, and, most important, in apathy on the part of many Oriental immigrants toward the school and its role as a factor in raising their standard of living, building the social life of their own community, and integrating them with the old-timer community. (E4)

INDOCTRINATION

The indoctrinative character of the educational trends is most detrimental to the development of the Israeli youth, especially of its Oriental sector.

Criticizing the education system in Israel, Levin says: "Our education is full of propaganda and persuasion. The result is an immature pupil who can be easily persuaded. . . . Our education is based on hypnotism rather than on critical thinking." (L1:51)

The teacher in this trend system indoctrinates pupils with ready-made answers. Obviously these students do not learn to be interested in the ways in which people make up their minds, are not willing to examine problems from various points of view, and are not encouraged to look at their own interests, prejudices, and allegiances. It can hardly be expected that this type of education will produce mature citizens who are able to reach some workable consensus in the present divided society.

The Oriental child, whose experience of democratic living is more limited than that of the Ashkenazi, is liable to be more adversely influenced by this indoctrinative education.

In various ways, then, examination of the trend system in the light of the ethnic problem shows that it is an obstacle on the road to social integration.

Needed Research

Present research on the Oriental youth in the school touches only the periphery of the problem, leaving more basic issues untouched.

The reluctance of the Israeli to admit that there is a serious lack of mutual ethnic participation in the country, and the greater unwillingness of the educator to face this problem at school, may be the major reasons for lack of research in this area.

Such reluctance not only fails to accomplish anything but is also dangerous. Studies which will inform the public on the severity of the situation and which will examine the underlying factors of the problem must be the beginning of a more constructive attitude.

Educators must be encouraged to undertake systematic study of *the extent of school segregation* on the local and national levels. Special attention should be paid not only to the psychological attitudes of the residents of the community involved but to *all conditions which indirectly strengthen segregation.* The extent to which ecological factors, school zoning, the establishment of special schools for new immigrants, and the "trends" of education aggravate the situation should be examined systematically.

Studies focused on the problem of the Oriental child in the school proper should parallel those conducted in the wider community. One major area for research should center around the problem of the *conflicting values of the Ashkenazim and the Orientals.* These questions await an answer: What is the difference between the educational expectations of the two ethnic groups? Does the school follow the set of values held by one group while ignoring those of the other group? Do the parents in both groups feel that the school fulfills the task of transmitting to their children the values which they cherish?

The *degree of conflict between the school expectations of the two groups* can be studied by direct inquiry of representatives of both groups. It can also be observed through the study of the *relationships between the Ashkenazi teacher and the Oriental parent.* Does the Oriental parent find the teacher helpful, or is the Ashkenazi teacher seen as an authoritarian to be avoided? Does the Oriental parent feel comfortable in the school, or does he consider himself inferior? Is he willing to contribute his skills and resources, or does he feel that he has nothing to offer? Does the teacher view the Oriental parent as an equal? Does the teacher blame the Oriental parent for the failure of the Oriental child to conform to the school expectations? Does the teacher approach the Oriental parent for help?

The *relationship between the Oriental teacher and the Oriental parent* presents another important area for research. It may be worth while to find out whether the Oriental teacher is better able to understand the Oriental parent. Does the Oriental parent find more support in a teacher who belongs to his own group, or is the relationship between these two similar to that between the Ashkenazi teacher and the Oriental parent? Does the Oriental teacher identify with the values of the Ashkenazi group? If such identification exists, at what emotional expense is it achieved, and how does it influence his attitude toward the Oriental child?

Relationships between Ashkenazi and Oriental pupils are an unexplored and ignored area—a situation characteristic of an educational philosophy which is mainly interested in the amount of subject matter accumulated by students rather than in the quality of the human relationships prevalent in the school.

Do class values or ethnic prejudices operate in children just as they do in the life of their parents and their community?

There is only one study dealing with this problem in Israel. Fuah (F12) found through sociometric techniques that ethnic and socioeconomic origin are factors which influence the status of children in an inter-ethnic kindergarten.

Studies in America also give an affirmative answer to this question; they show that group consciousness and social prejudices are fairly well developed by five years of age, (R2) that they are direct reflections of family and neighborhood values, and that the child tends to accept adult values and interpretations with little modification. (H7)

The social taboo against probing ethnic attitudes in people in general, and in young children especially, is very strong. Therefore, projective research techniques will be more advantageous than a direct approach in this area. (T10, H7)

Research is needed on the effects of these attitudes on the behavior and inter-ethnic relations of pupils as manifested in preferences, rejections, and grouping in a mixed class. A related question is: Do Oriental pupils show the same attitude and behavior toward the Ashkenazim, as the Ashkenazim do toward the Orientals?

A sociometric study of the relationships between Negro and white pupils in mixed classes in America (K6) shows that white boys and girls favored the members of their own group at the second grade level and that this self-preference tendency increased gradually with age. By the tenth grade there was almost no crossing of color lines by the white children. The Negro pupils from grade two to six chose white children just about as often as Negro pupils, but by the tenth grade they also kept almost entirely to themselves.

Observation of the interrelationships among pupils in school and in out-of-school activities, interviewing, and sociometric techniques (J2) might prove most helpful in determining the prevalence of these conditions among Israeli students.

A research area of great importance is *the psychological dynamics underlying ethnic attitudes among children*. Are these attitudes a part of the personality structure? Is a more intolerant child also "more constricted, cynical, fearful, less confident and secure, and more suspicious and ethnocentric than children of greater tolerance?" (G4:91) Is there a positive relationship between authoritarian parents and prejudiced children and between democratic home atmosphere and non-prejudiced children? (H3)

The role of the non-state-supported traditional school (called Kutab or Heder) in the life of the Oriental community also needs to be studied. (E6, S3) Some areas for investigation are:

The percentage of Oriental children who attend these schools.

The importance of these institutions to the Oriental parents and their effects on parent-child relations.

The attitude of the children toward the ethnic school and teachers.

The curriculum of the ethnic school and its educational and psychological effects.

Summary

This chapter analyzed some of the major curricular and administrative principles of the school system—school zoning, the "trend" system, and promotion policies—in the light of the ethnic problem. The discussion showed that these major policies have resulted in some adverse effects on the growth of the Oriental pupil and on the development of sound ethnic group relations.

Three factors in the school status of the Oriental pupil were discussed, and the analysis led to certain conclusions:

1. The claim that low intelligence is responsible for the failure of the Oriental pupil is only partly correct.

2. Behind this failure lies the Israeli social system. One source of failure of the Oriental child seems to be that he is a lower-class child in a middle-class school.

3. The subject-matter curriculum is the *major cause* of the failure of the Oriental pupil. The laudable efforts of the school system to help the Orientals raise their status have proved partly abortive, mainly because of the failure of the academic curriculum to furnish the Oriental child with the needed motivation for continuous efforts to improve his own life and his own community through education.

With due respect to the great achievements of the Israeli school system, we are led to the conclusion that in many cases the school is a source of new ethnic tensions, rather than a means to the improvement of the ethnic group relations.

X

The Role of the School

It is the purpose of this chapter to delineate the role of the school as an agent for improving ethnic group relations in Israel. In the light of its proper objectives in this role, certain characteristics of an adequate school program will be discussed, and possibilities for curriculum features suggested.

Objectives

Our analysis of the impact of the cultural contact in Israel suggests that the school has certain important obligations:

1. To help raise the socio-economic standard of living and the educational level of the Orientals, and to facilitate the productivization and normalization of their occupational structure.

2. To fight the conditions of anomie in the Oriental community, the tension in the family, and the marginality among the youth.

3. To bring the people, especially the youth, of the two communities into "participation on an equal basis" in order that they will build inter-ethnic primary groups, learn to respect each other's cultural norms, and gradually construct a new culture based on the values of the two communities.

No one of these objectives can be achieved as an isolated unit. They should be understood as interrelated aspects, rather than sequential steps, and should permeate every part of the program of improving ethnic group relations through the school.

125

Democratization of the School

The school has to adjust to the character and needs of all pupils, including the Orientals. Israeli educators are aware of this need. However, the application of this principle so far has resulted mainly in planning for homogeneous grouping and semi-annual promotion policies. (B11, R3, E13, B8)

Homogeneous grouping, it should be realized, will result in the relegation of the majority of the Oriental pupils to the slow sections and will severely decrease opportunities for inter-ethnic participation.

Opposing homogeneous grouping in American schools, Davis says:

> Homogeneous grouping really sets up different social and cultural groups within the school, and thus establishes different learning environment. The result is that most of the middle class groups and most of the lower class groups lose something. Segregated from each other, unable therefore either to stimulate or to imitate each other, each group fails to learn well the activities and insights in which the other group excel. (D3:96)

No attempt to disguise the nature of the sections will deceive the pupils or the public. Their notion will be that the slow sections are composed of "dumb Orientals." The demoralizing effect of such a policy on ethnic relations cannot be overemphasized.

Another major objection to the plan of homogeneous grouping is that it will segregate the potential leaders from the masses. This point has special implications for this era of "crisis of pioneering Zionism" and needs some elaboration.

Criticicizing the present ego-ideal—the pioneer—and raising a new ideal of leadership and service, Frankenstein says:

> The pioneer assumes a national task and he accomplishes it by himself. He marches ahead of the camp, rather than working with it. . . . In contrast to the pioneer, the democratic leader works with the people for the fulfillment of the task. . . . This new ego ideal calls for a change in education from emphasis on the national aspiration of building a homeland, to emphasis on the importance of the individual, and on sensitivity toward the feelings of others. (F5:204)

It is questionable whether segregation of the bright pupils—many of them future leaders—will prepare them for this new role. Democratic leadership can be learned only through living with the average pupils, understanding their needs, learning their norms of behavior, and sometimes even "following" them. Lewin says: "What holds for the education of democratic followers, also holds true for the education of democratic leaders. It seems that both roles have to be learned if either one is to be played well." (L3:199) And pupils will find it most difficult to learn these two functions of leadership in a homogeneous class.

The few Oriental students in the homogeneous "bright section" have the best chance of becoming future leaders of the Oriental community. However, given the present educational conditions, it is highly questionable whether these young Orientals will be able or ready to go back to their people and work with them. Simon says: "There are many potential leaders among the immigrants. . . . The majority of them, however, are not ready to serve their community. They utilize their abilities to get away from their communal origins and to assimilate in the community of the old-timers." (I3:60)

Only through friendly living with the average Oriental, and through working on the problems of the Oriental group, is there hope that these potential leaders will develop a sense of belongingness and of responsibility to work for the improvement of their people.

We conclude, therefore, that the plan to reduce school failure through establishment of homogeneous grouping must be rejected on the ground that it will lead to segregation of pupils according to ethnic origin, and will jeopardize the development of democratic leadership.

The proponents of homogeneous grouping might accept these objections but continue to argue that the failure of the Oriental pupil in the heterogeneous group is much more detrimental than the harm caused by homogeneous grouping. Observing a heterogeneous first grade, Shur says:

> In the beginning of the year the Oriental children realized that a wide discrepancy existed between the wealth of information that their Ashkenazi peers had and what they themselves knew. They considered themselves inferior and refrained from taking any active part in learning in order to avoid further failure.
>
> We may assume that if these children were in a homogeneous group where severe competition was minimized, they would be much more successful in their studies. (S4:159)

This argument is valid if considered within the framework of the present subject-matter curriculum. Within this framework the establishment of homogeneous grouping may be the only way of reducing the failure of the Oriental pupil. The policy of homogeneous grouping is an attempt to remedy the symptoms of a problem without getting at their source. The answer to the problem may lie in abandoning the grade-standard theory and in democratization of the school practices and the adaptation of the curriculum to individual and cultural differences.

The school has to provide every child with the opportunity to experience success and achieve a sense of accomplishment. Success furnishes the motivation for continuous search, exploration, and learning. A child can experience success only if the school curriculum meets his needs and interests.

The school should operate as a miniature community full of problems to be solved and things to be done. Each individual child will read, write, compute, talk, and draw about meanings derived from his own experience. The three R's will become a means of establishing communication and relationship with others, and an instrument for solving immediate on-going problems, rather than an end in themselves, or a skill to be learned for use in the future.

The idea that children should have a major role in the selection of the problems to be studied and in planning the activities by which the problems may be solved is a basic principle in modern education. This does not mean that the teacher has no right to try to develop interest or initiate activities. What the teacher has no right to do is to compel or manipulate the students to follow his pre-planned activities. There is a basic difference between an attempt to offer a choice of opportunities, which could be modified, developed, or even rejected by students, and scheming to bring about predetermined outcomes through predesigned programs.

Assuming that the curriculum is to be based on the felt needs and concerns of pupils, and that the role of the teacher is to guide and promote the growth of the learner, cooperative pupil- teacher planning becomes the most essential part of the day's work. Kelley says:

> Planning what you are going to do is essential if you are to follow your own purposes. . . . Planning is the tentative layout of the assault on a problem. . . . It is almost universally omitted when knowledge is set out to be learned.
>
> Planning can of course be done alone, but it usually involves other

people. . . . The process of getting group agreement on what is to be done, deciding who will do the separate parts, and what the first attack shall be is the essence of cooperation. It is a group experience children must have if they are to learn to work together outside of school. (K1:86)

The following illustration of the steps through which a classroom activity might proceed, adapted from an outline prepared by the Philadelphia Public Schools, (P4) shows that cooperative planning should permeate every aspect of the program rather than merely the selection of the problem to be studied.

A. The project is initiated.

A rich, meaningful experience, or series of experiences, such as reading a story, making a trip, or an important event in the community or school, should stimulate appropriate thinking and activity on the part of the pupils. Such an experience is preliminary to teacher-pupil planning. It motivates the pupils to raise questions on the subject and be interested in pursuing it further.

B. The objectives of the project are formulated.

The objectives are planned cooperatively. A general discussion and some reading and exploration of the subject might lead the class to a decision to drop the project or to pursue it further.

C. The project is organized.

The teacher and students select the specific topic. The title can be changed as the project develops, and should be regarded as tentative. The various aspects of the project are formulated, and the responsibility for their elaboration and study is delegated to various committees, or to the class as a whole.

D. The project is developed.

Committees or individuals investigate various sources of information, such as books, maps, resource people, and excursions. They organize the accumulated data and present "progress reports" to the whole group. In the light of these reports the objectives and organization of the project will be modified.

E. The project is brought to a conclusion.

Some form of culminating activity should conclude the study. It helps to tie the project together and provides immeasurable satisfaction for a job well done. The feeling of having done something useful becomes stronger when the experience is shared with others. The culminating activity may be in the form of an exhibit for the school and the community, an assembly program, or an article in the school or community paper.

F. The project is evaluated.

When people work cooperatively on a project they develop a sense of need to evaluate their own progress, departing from the well-known notion that evaluation is "the teacher's business." Evaluation should be continuous and cooperative. The individual pupil, the small committee, and the whole class should learn to stop from time to time and evaluate the progress of their work not only in terms of growth in knowledge and basic skills, but also in terms of the behavior of and the interaction among the various participants. Skills in group process and sensitivity in human relations should be emphasized and examined even in the primary grades. This approach to evaluation is a constructive tool and an integral part of cooperative planning rather than a threat to students.

Tests may be taken by the student individually and on his own initiative. The test plays a constructive role only in an atmosphere where academic failure and competitive grades do not exist, and where the individual is judged according to the best he can do, rather than according to a predetermined grade standard. In an atmosphere where individual differences are recognized and accepted, the student will feel free to take a test as a measure of self-evaluation in the subject-matter area exactly as one takes a periodic physical examination.

It should be noted that the above outline of the steps through which a class project may proceed is not a model to be followed literally. It is only a general framework for operation, which must be changed and filled in by the teacher according to a specific situation. However, the fragmented, teacher-dominated, day-by-day type of instruction should be discontinued and replaced by a long-range cooperative program.

The recognition that students are not statistical averages and cannot be expected to achieve the same grade standard is a prerequisite for a program of improving ethnic group relations through the school. The curriculum must provide for individual differences in abilities and interests, and accept the fact that each pupil will have somewhat different achievements. The individualization of curriculum experiences is qualitative as well as quantitative.

> The emphasis in the subject curriculum usually is to bring everybody up to the minimum acceptable standard which is primarily quantitative in conception. Individualization is in terms of rate and quantity of learning. . . . In the modern curriculum individuality is highly prized.

> While attempting to insure common understanding and skills, emphasis is placed on helping each learner to extend and improve his personal uniqueness, so that instead of all engaging in the same kinds of experience, all have unique experiences while cooperatively attacking common problems. Emphasis is on quality of learning. (E10:72)

The program of the modern school is not limited to teaching children academic knowledge and scholastic skills. It includes learnings and the development of appreciations in many areas not touched by the old school curriculum.

Pupils of high intelligence tend to do well in arithmetic, reading, and the social studies. However, intelligence seems to play a much smaller role in such important areas of learning as esthetics and arts, shop activities, musical skills, spiritual values, and human relations skills.

Basic to the idea of distributing talent, rather than concentrating it, is the belief that children learn from one another as well as from the teacher or from instructional materials. Therefore, from the standpoint of pupil achievement there are advantages in grouping children in such a fashion that a cross section of the pupil population will be represented in each class.

With the foregoing in mind, it seems logical to suggest that our schools desist from emphasizing so much the rate of learning and emphasize instead the quality of the growth of their pupils. The eight-year period of the elementary school should constitute a period of continuous progress for each pupil at his own individual rate. Students should be promoted from grade to grade without the unrealistic expectation that all will have achieved a yearly grade standard. Being in a grade should not mean having reached any fixed standard, but rather having been in a school a certain length of time and having attained achievement proportionate to one's ability.

It is encouraging to note that the adoption of a "continuous progress" plan in New York City resulted in the reduction of the non-promotion figures from 9 per cent in the year 1925 to 0.8 per cent in 1950.

(A3:13) This change in promotion policies became a cornerstone in the movement of modern education. Says Elsbree: "There is nothing that will more compel people to think about the needs of children than the necessity of providing for them." (E11:432)

Faced with a tremendous problem of non-promotion, which has most detrimental effects on the ethnic problem, we definitely recommend the abolishment of the non-promotion policy and the establishment of a "continuous progress" plan. This administrative change will serve as an impetus for educators and laymen to re-examine the philosophy of the school, in order to adapt the curriculum to the needs of every child, including the Oriental child.

When these concepts of modern education come to permeate the school program, there is hope that the reservations of many educators and laymen concerning the desirability of grouping together "slow" and "normal" learners will be mitigated, or even completely disappear.

The Ashkenazi parent will come to understand that as a result of a program which provides for individual differences, the academic progress of his child will not be hampered by the existence of an academically slower group in the same classroom. On the contrary, his child will be enriched by an "educational osmosis" which occurs in a situation where a variety of personality and cultural types are housed in the same room.

The Oriental parent will come to understand that the welfare of his child is not going to be hampered by being together with Ashkenazi pupils who are academically brighter. On the contrary, his child will have an opportunity to learn to work together with the Ashkenazim as an equal and respected member and can overcome his feelings of ethnic strangeness.

The same can be said with regard to the problem of school zoning. There is hope that the various communities will awake to the need of establishing school zoning based on mutual ethnic association. The opposition of some segments of the Ashkenazi and Oriental community to such zoning will be alleviated if the public becomes convinced that the new arrangement will not lower the academic standard of the "good" schools and will not bring failure and frustrations to the slow learner.

A comprehensive analysis of modern education is beyond the scope of this paper. Some general principles have been discussed; others will be dealt with later. The major point to be emphasized is that democratization of the curriculum and the organization of the school is a basic and integral part of any program for improving ethnic group relations through education.

Vocational Education

The difficulty of integrating the Ashkenazi with the Oriental community stems not only from ethnic, but also from socio-economic origins. Vocational education should play a major role in widening the channels of socio-economic mobility and in normalizing the occupational structure of the Orientals.

Some of the most effective ways of fulfilling these objectives may be outlined as follows:

1. Establishing institutions for vocational education according to the needs of the specific community—for instance, vocational high schools, extension courses, vocational centers attached to factories and other business enterprises, and cooperative programs of work and study. (L6, R3) There is a serious shortage of vocational institutions, especially for girls. (E12)

2. Establishing institutions which will prepare for a wide range of vocations. (E12) The present vocational schools specialize mainly in the metal and electric branches.

3. Building a positive attitude toward vocational education. At present, the vocational institution is seen by many parents as a "second-rate" school where the child "who does not want to learn" is sent. Recognition of the vocational high school by the University will help in changing the negative attitude.

4. Experimenting with integrating vocational training with the other aspects of school work and attempting to introduce pre-vocational studies and experiences into the elementary school curriculum.

5. Seeing vocational guidance as a continuous and cooperative process which constitutes an integral part of vocational information. At the present such guidance is based mainly on some testing by outside agencies which do not have continuous contact with the students, teachers, and parents. Vocational information is a subject which is rarely taught at school.

6. Establishing funds with the specific purpose of helping the Oriental student achieve a high vocational status.

7. Mobilizing business and labor organizations to support and pro-

mote vocational education. At present, the business circles are doing very little in this area. (E12)

8. Enacting child labor laws which protect the juvenile without limiting his opportunities for vocational training and work experiences. (K9)

The Study of Ethnic Group Problems

The democratization of the school curriculum and a more realistic and meaningful education are prerequisites for the improvement of ethnic group relations. In addition, the teacher must aim at developing desirable intergroup attitudes and relations through a *direct program* based on the study of ethnic group problems.

These problems are being neglected in the overwhelming majority of the Israeli schools. It is our contention that the suggestion to introduce this theme in the school will meet strong opposition. The rationale of the opponents may be that the school should emphasize activities in which members of all cultural groups unite and should stress the similarities of human needs and emotions rather than studying the problem of prejudice and ethnic tension.

Study shows that many teachers in America are opposed to the direct approach. One argues thus:

> My third graders accept differences in color, creed and national background without a qualm. They learn together, play together and eat together apparently unconscious of the prejudices we adults take so seriously. Should I be the first to arouse their sense of being different from one another racially and religiously? (V2:83)

We definitely agree that the importance of bringing the members of the various ethnic groups to work together on a common cause cannot be overemphasized. This does not mean, however, that the teacher can bury his head in the school sand and pretend that ethnic strangeness does not exist in our society. It may be that a specific sheltered group of Ashkenazi children is not aware of these tensions. However, the school cannot ignore its task of preparing this group to deal intelligently with the ethnic problem in the future.

Assuming that the ethnic problem should be frankly recognized and critically studied in the school and that various aspects of this theme can be adapted to the level of understanding of any age group, we now proceed to suggest some principles and programs for the study of the ethnic problem at the school.

PRINCIPLES

Intergroup education throughout the curriculum. Intergroup education should permeate every aspect of the curriculum rather than become a new "subject." Opportunities to encourage intergroup understanding may come during study of language arts, social studies, science, or nutrition, in celebrations, or in any other part of the curriculum.

There is a place in the curriculum for units on intergroup themes which endeavor to impart true information, to correct prevalent misconceptions, and to analyze the socio-psychological basis of prejudice. There is a place, too, for units where the ethnic problem appears as an integral part of more inclusive social situations—units on education, neighborhoods, employment, recreation, and welfare agencies, for instance.

The need for a multiple approach. An effective program of developing desirable intergroup attitudes should utilize many kinds of activities and approaches, rather than rely upon a single approach. Obtaining information through reading about the Iraqi or Yemenite Jews (i.e., about their history, ceremonies, and contributions to the Israeli culture), for instance, is not a sufficiently effective approach. Prejudice stems only in part from misinformation, and consequently activities which do more than provide information are needed.

> Where reading and discussion, intergroup contacts, joint participation in common holiday observances, role playing and other approaches are utilized there is greater likelihood that hostility will be reduced and desirable attitudes shaped. Such a multiple approach provides the pupil with opportunity to read for information, to discuss his feelings about others who are different, to work with various groups and to play out experiences which have been sources of tension. (S8:59)

A survey, made in 1947, of the Detroit public schools (E1) revealed as many as eleven approaches to intergroup education. In his report of the study, the author discusses the strengths and limitations of every practice and recommends that the program of intergroup education be based on a variety of approaches rather than on a single approach.

The need for a realistic program. A program of intergroup education should be realistic rather than "sugar-coated" and "romantic." Criticism of intercultural programs in America shows that it

> seems still in large degree to function safely upon a non-controversial if not at times almost sentimental plane. Emphasis seems weighted heavily upon the customs and cultural contributions of various groups and races. . . . Emphasis upon the civilization of yesterday, while justifiable when related to a larger whole, may preclude facing the controversial problems of today and tomorrow. There is not much awareness of the economic roots of intercultural conflicts. (B9:58)

A constructive program avoids overemphasizing the "quaint" or antique aspects of a minority culture. For instance, the study of the Golden Age of the Jews in Spain may have no effect on the attitude of the Ashkenazi student toward the inhabitants of the Sephardic section in his community.

A realistic program should tackle the problem of the lower-class status of many sectors of the Oriental community. The Kurd Jew, for example, is not by nature ignorant or dirty; it is a lower-class position which has deprived so many of his tribe of opportunities for more education and of better facilities for cleanliness.

A realistic program does not minimize differences in the values (such as work, achievement, or cleanliness) held by the various groups. The point that basic values such as friendliness, honesty, and moral courage are shared by all should be emphasized. (S8)

A realistic program calls for study of the dynamics underlying the behavior of the minority group member. The most obvious effect of prejudice is seen in the person against whom the prejudice is directed. Withdrawal or aggressive behavior may be rooted in ethnic insecurity, family tension, marginality, and prejudice.

Ethnic tensions and conflicts tend to focus in certain problem areas such as labor exchange, social welfare, housing, governmental benefits, or school population. A realistic program should diagnose these tension spots and examine them in the light of their relation to the ethnic problem.

Acceptance of group belongingness. An effective program should help the minority group pupil accept his group belonging. The "hush-hush" policy of not mentioning minority group membership should be replaced by a program which encourages these members to capitalize on the cultural contributions of their respective groups. As Trager and Radke say,

If children are to accept or reject persons on their merits and themselves be similarly treated, then group membership of persons must be acknowledged and accepted also. This is possible when group membership is viewed without prejudice or misconceptions, does not determine one's status per se, and is not a topic which is taboo and avoided. (T10:240)

The student should be helped to avoid visualizing the various ethnic groups in terms of stereotypes, and should learn to realize that no group is all black or all white, but that each has its lights and shadows.

The need for social vision. An effective program should inspire the students with social consciousness and readiness to help and rehabilitate the disintegrating sectors of the Israeli community.

Education in Israel has succeeded in inspiring youth with love for their country and with an aspiration for rebuilding it. The youth are fully aware that the country is poor in natural resources. This realization, however, does not result in attitudes of dislike toward the poor land. On the contrary, the youth are imbued with the determination and conviction that their task is to rebuild and beautify it. This determination is expressed in one of the most typical Israeli songs, with its promise to the land: "We shall dress thee in a garment of cement and we shall clothe thee with a carpet of gardens."

This positive attitude and philosophy should be instilled in the youth not only with regard to the land but also with regard to its people. It is a fact that poverty, ignorance, superstition, and authoritarian behavior are prevalent among some segments of the Israeli community. The inference, however, is not that these sectors should be despised or looked down upon. On the contrary, the inference is that they constitute virgin ground—an area of potential growth. The development and rehabilitation of this area will succeed only if the builders approach its inhabitants with much love, patience, respect, and social vision.

Emphasis on school and community problems. A comprehensive program should deal with the intergroup problems of the specific class or school, and also with those of the wider community. Putting emphasis only on the ethnic problems prevalent in the community fails to relate them to the daily experiences of the students at school and fails to modify their behavior. Emphasizing only the school problems fails

to show them in the broader context of the deep cleavages in our contemporary social structure.

Working on intergroup problems in the school and in the community
requires the cooperation and participation of parents and community
leaders. The use of parents and community members as resource people
might provide many children with security and satisfaction in their own
and others' group membership. In particular, the participation of
Oriental citizens in the school program will contribute toward a positive
affirmation of minority group membership and toward improved relations with Ashkenazi students.

PROGRAMS

The study of the community. The study of the community has un-
limited possibilities for intergroup education. Even in kindergarten,
children can learn to perceive the neighborhood as multi-cultured and
to accept the different people who live in it as neighbors. The teacher
should foster pleasant experiences with members of different groups, so
that the children will come to accept the differences as right and good.
Dolls, in addition, might serve to represent the various groups of the
community, and reactions of children to these dolls can be utilized in
order to initiate discussion. (S8)

It is common practice for primary grade children to make a map of
the community based on a number of field trips. They identify and
locate big and small neighborhood landmarks and can share what they
know about the various ethnic groups represented in the district.

The primary grade child is conscious of the differences in housing
and neighborhoods. The problem is how to teach him not to associate
poor living conditions with badness. Causes of failure should be
analyzed according to the level of understanding of the specific group of
children. The higher elementary grades can delve into the complex
problem of the unequal opportunities of the poor and the various
practices which perpetuate a low standard of living for certain groups.

Seeing conditions which need correction, such as the slums which
breed sickness and delinquency, will help students learn that our democracy is not perfect. The analysis of the shadows in our social structure
should be approached constructively, by raising such questions as these:
What is done? What could be done? What can we, as students, do to
alleviate these conditions? Students will come to realize in this way

that democracy is something which can grow and that its growth depends on the understanding and support of every citizen.

Tours of housing projects, union offices, and welfare agencies is a means of teaching children about organized attempts to improve the standard of living in the community. Older children may intern in these social agencies (R5, H5) and learn through firsthand experience of the problems involved in social reconstruction and rehabilitation—problems such as the demoralizing effects of philanthropy, the difficulty of generating leadership in the helped group, and the need for reciprocal relations of give and take.

A related topic is the attitude toward various kinds of work. In our culture, economic improvement is widely identified with moral improvement. The middle-class values of material success should be replaced by more humane and spiritual ones, such as cooperativeness, tolerance, and the satisfaction of doing a good job or rendering a faithful service.

Children can begin in the primary grades to learn that character is not a function of such externals as clothing, housing, and occupation—that people are to be accepted for what they are rather than for the way they talk, the kind of clothes they wear, or the kind of house they live in. (S8) Older students can investigate more complicated problems, such as the need for the normalization of the economic structure of the Oriental community and the difficulties involved in adapting to a new economy. Projects for vocational training should be examined in terms of their contribution to the productivity of the Oriental and Ashkenazi workers. Of special importance is the study of the labor exchange and other employment agencies in order that students will understand their operation and not tend to rationalize failure to get a desired job as ethnic discrimination.

The question of inter-ethnic association in the school and in the community is an area which requires careful study. Close association and "participation on an equal basis" is not only a method, but also a goal, of intergroup education. Children of all age groups should learn to look for opportunities to increase these associations, and should learn to examine the various social institutions in terms of their ethnic composition.

In examining the patterns of association in a specific school, the following questions can be raised: Do some students like to work and play only with their own gang? Do well-to-do students exclude poor students from their groups? Do ethnic group members tend to associate only with their own group on the playground or in extracurricular activities? (V1)

Students can learn to increase mutual association in the school through developing more group activities, shifting or rotating committee membership, and bringing in the isolates. Children can find opportunities to know children different from themselves. When the school is too homogeneous in its ethnic composition, these associations can be found in schools located in other neighborhoods.

Exchange visits are valuable experiences during which students of various ethnic origins can share with each other units of work and special programs. Exchange visits between schools must be so planned that the visiting group shares in some activity. Visiting which offers no more than gazing at other children is not only a waste of time but is also harmful, particularly when the children of the two groups are of different backgrounds. (B6)

Older students may extend this study into the community. Through surveys, interviewing, and use of resource people they can investigate the following problems: What is the effect of the Yemenite quarter on the total life of the community? Why is there "voluntary segregation"? Is it really voluntary?

Visitation of public and cooperative housing projects raises many questions: Was the ethnic factor considered in their planning? How did it happen that the cooperative projects, despite being based on progressive social ideologies, rarely have non-Sephardic Oriental residents?

A study of the formal and informal associations may reveal the extent of intergroup participation and representation. Some questions for discussion are these: Is there an adequate representation of Orientals in the municipality? Can a charity or civic improvement organization reach the Oriental layman without having adequate representation of Orientals among its leaders? Do the youth of the community have inter-ethnic experiences in their out-of-school life, as in recreation, camping, and informal meeting places?

In brief, the foregoing discussion illustrates that a realistic study of the community can help in sensitizing students to ethnic problems and in preparing them to contribute their share toward better intergroup relations.

The study of the family. The study of the family is another avenue for helping students see and understand intergroup problems. Young children's ideas of what families are like—their size, composition, activities, and conveniences—are largely molded by their own family circumstances. Those belonging to small families assume all families are small; those living in cramped quarters with no privacy assume that crowded housing is normal. Older children soon realize that families differ in many respects. If the school has not recognized these variations, if reading and discussion have tended to establish one pattern as right, children are self-conscious if their own family deviates from this pattern, and begin to judge families as good or bad according to it.

The typical study at school is limited to the middle-class Ashkenazi family. Children whose families deviate from that pattern feel that there must be something wrong with them—that they have something to be ashamed of. Without explicit teaching about differences, without an effort to cultivate an understanding of reasons for these differences, and without a study of the wide range of family patterns in the Israeli society, unhappiness lies in store for many children.

Emphasis should be placed not only on the actions and behavior, but also on the feelings, of family members. For instance, when children learn that their fathers react one way when they are busy or tired and another way when they are free or rested, they may gain the first inkling of the concept of caused behavior. The socio-drama technique is an excellent means of helping students understand the dynamics of behavior of other family members. (T5)

If studies in family life are to contribute to intergroup understanding, they should be realistic. Many incidents occur in family living that annoy or upset family members. Diagnosis of these sources of friction (T1) will reveal to the teacher many areas of needed study.

> One fifth grade teacher discussed with her class situations at home that especially annoyed them. They used a series of sociodramas to develop alternate ways of behaving and then analyzed each to determine whether it overcame the difficulty and what effect it had on the feelings of those involved. (T2:60)

Gaining insight into the feelings and motivations of family members and gaining skill in handling conflicts in the family is of special help to the marginal Oriental child. It helps the child understand the adjustment problems of his parents and appreciate the emotional security, guidance, and cultural enrichment he can receive at home.

The school can play an important role in building solidarity and cohesiveness in the family. This can be done by working not only with the children but also with their parents. Any attempt to help the Oriental children without guiding their parents may create tense relations between the two generations by portraying the Ashkenazi instructors as symbols of progress and the Oriental parents as symbols of backwardness. (O4)

The education and the gradual transformation of the total family is the only way of delivering it from inner strife and tension. Consequently, the school must make every effort to create an atmosphere such that the Oriental parents will want to come to the school and share in its activities with their children. Some methods of working toward this goal are (1) use of parents as resource people, (2) cooperative planning with parents, (3) P.T.A. activities adapted to the level of interest of every group, (4) family camping, trips, and picnics under the school's auspices, (5) parent-child courses, forums, and discussion groups, (6) conferences with and visits of teachers, and (7) experiences in "family celebrations" (to be discussed later).

In brief, the school can help in building mutual understanding and good will between parents and children and in lessening the difficulties caused by divergent ideas and standards of conduct.

The study of holidays. All children need to know and appreciate their cultural heritage. The need is most acute in the case of those children who are ashamed of their origin, their parents, or their poverty. When a child loses his self-respect and fails to feel satisfaction in being accepted by the group in which he finds himself, he may be on the way to maladjustment and delinquency. Emotional stability and mental health depend upon self-respect. The child who is afflicted with self-hate cannot be expected to respect others.

Programs should be developed which attempt to familiarize the pupil with the different cultural backgrounds of the Israeli people, and make him more appreciative of the contributions made by many people of various ethnic origins to our present life. The celebration of the Jewish holidays is an excellent illustration of how this principle may be implemented in the school.

The celebration of the holidays is one of the most impressive and refreshing events in the Israeli school. However, the emphasis is mainly on traditions of Biblical times and on modern interpretations of these holidays. There is a de-emphasizing of the traditions of the Ashkenazi Diaspora; and the traditions and customs of Oriental Jewry are almost completely ignored. These two phenomena are a consequence of an educational philosophy which rejects the values of the life of the Jew in exile and ignores the fact of ethnic differences. The traditions and customs of both Ashkenazi and Oriental Jews in the Diaspora are, however, an unexplored resource which can enrich the celebration of the holidays and create more identification with the Jewish people and culture, and bring children and parents closer.

The Ashkenazi teachers are handicapped in their work with the Oriental pupils and community by not knowing their customs and traditions. It is the task of pre- and in-service education programs to help the teacher overcome this handicap.

The Oriental or Ashkenazi parent will enjoy coming to school and participating in a celebration which revives his childhood experiences in the Diaspora. The parent can become a resource person who helps the school plan the celebrations "the way they used to do it back home," and can even participate actively in entertaining the audience.

Singing songs and using non-Hebrew expressions in the mother tongue of the parents will make the celebrations a much more attractive event and will serve to strengthen school-home and child-parent relations.

At present the school overemphasizes big celebrations where the whole school celebrates or several schools celebrate together. Often the individual child feels lost in these big ceremonies.

In the process of transforming the orientation of the Jewish holidays from one of religious ceremonial to one of secular, agricultural, and national celebration, the Israeli people created new forms for community celebrations—forms such as marching with torches, and bringing the first fruits to the Jewish National Fund.

This modern interpretation of the holidays failed, however, to create new forms of celebration for the family. The holiday, well noted for its unifying effect on the Jewish family, is gradually losing this important role. The lack of family ceremonies is especially detrimental for the Oriental families, many of whom do not identify as strongly as do the Ashkenazi with the larger community.

In aiming to strengthen and enrich family life, the school should provide experiences in ways of celebrating holidays in the family circle.

For instance, before the Passover, parents may be invited to have the Seder with their children at school. Instead of, or in addition to, the usual arrangement, where parents sit in a corner and watch the children's performance, the parents mingle with small groups of children. Many Seders based on the traditions of the various sub-cultures may go on simultaneously. This approach to holiday celebrations at school creates a family atmosphere, provides an opportunity to experience the traditions of another culture, helps the child accept his own cultural origin, and strengthens parent-child relations.

The building up of self-regard in a minority group through helping its members to identify with their ethnic tradition is a point of controversy in American literature. Frequently an intercultural program emphasizes differences unnecessarily, and the effect can be regressive and aid in perpetuating stereotypes. Heaton says that minority group children "often feel that they become an exhibition of foreign ways and that in doing so they lose their identity as young American citizens and students." (H4:21)

Krech thinks that

> To present Negroes or Mexicans or Chinese or Jews in the context of special groups with special dress, special songs and special foods is presenting them in the wrong context. They should be presented in their context of functional groups and as American groups. (K8:522)

This criticism is very serious. Teachers should find ways of utilizing the cultural diversity represented in the school without giving students a sense of being set apart. The problem is one of finding a balance between presenting the minorities as "special" groups and presenting them as "functional" groups. Neither too much nor too little emphasis on the "special" group is desirable.

Another point to be considered in planning celebrations is to avoid "minstrel shows" which portray a minority group in a stereotype or in a ridiculous light. Our observation shows that there are already a few attempts to present the Yemenite and Kurdistan groups as naive and to ridicule their accent. Teachers should be aware of the different interpretations placed upon minstrel shows and recognize that what is meant as a joke by one ethnic group is thought of as an insult and humiliation by another group.

The study of religion. In studying religious differences among the ethnic groups, the starting point may be the differences existing among the students in the specific classroom. Children may learn that some families attend Ashkenazi synagogues, some Sephardi, and some Yemenite, and that some do not attend a synagogue at all. They can find out the similarities and differences among the religious customs, prayers, ways of reading aloud from the Torah, and other synagogue rituals of the various groups.

The students should be helped to understand that what seems strange to them is natural to others and what seems natural to them is strange to others.

Even first graders can appreciate the fact that we must learn to accept and respect differences in others as we want others to accept and respect the ways in which we differ from them, provided the learning experiences are at their level. (S8:101)

The idea that people should be allowed to be different is not promoted sufficiently by the school. With respect to the religious aspect of this problem, observation indicates that the schools of the religious "trend" do not provide any understanding of the beliefs and feelings of the non-Orthodox or non-religious people, and seldom provide understanding of the Orientals' synagogues and their religious customs. The other schools ignore the subject of religion almost completely. For the Oriental children, the majority of whom have religious parents, this means that they learn a great deal about the strategy of the Israeli army in the war of the Maccabees but learn hardly any prayers, chants from the Torah, or other religious rituals, which are the daily experiences of their family life.

The foregoing analysis leads to the conclusion that in the controversial area of religion the role of the school is twofold: to promote knowledge of the religious life of the various ethnic groups; and to promote mutual respect among the Orthodox, non-Orthodox, and non-religious segments of the population.

The study of history. History naturally lends itself to intercultural study. However, the present course of study places undue emphasis on the history of the Ashkenazi Jews, neglecting the history of the Oriental Jews. The teacher interested in intercultural education has the responsibility for correcting this without going to the opposite extreme.

The question to be raised is this: What kind of history teaching is going to help the students to identify with people different from them, and to understand their problems and difficulties?

Criticizing the present approach to the teaching of history, which emphasizes mainly the negative aspects of the life of the Jews in exile, Rieger says:

> We have to teach our children about the Jews in the Diaspora, their way of life, works of art, problems, and hopes. They have to learn that there are not only shadows but also lights in the life of the Diaspora. It is unreasonable to paint a dark picture of Jewish life in exile and then expect the students to identify themselves with our people abroad. (R3:250)

Only an approach to history which sensitizes students to human problems and values, and shows light as well as shadow, in many ways of life is conducive to intercultural understanding.

The study of geography. Geography is another subject area which can be utilized for promoting intergroup relations. According to the present course of study, the higher elementary grades study almost all the countries of the world. However, the school seldom makes use of the fact that the people of Israel come from more than sixty countries. How real geography becomes when a student's mother comes to class to tell about the life of the Jewish community in her country of origin, or displays some objects characteristic of that land. And the student who is a new immigrant, telling of his experiences in the land of his origin, becomes a center of interest and finds a place in the group.

Higher grades may study the impact of the cultures of foreign lands on their Jewish communities and the various contributions of these Jewish groups to the Israeli culture.

The study of literature. A challenging task confronting modern Israeli literature is the description of the new Ashkenazi and Oriental immigrants. Literature should present the story of immigration in terms of human experience and as an aid to the understanding of the attitudes and relationships of our heterogeneous population.

Present literature, especially juvenile, deals with the "old" immigration mainly in terms of the Zionist task. The immigrants are portrayed as "builders who blazed the roads for future generations," or as pioneers who "in the desolate spaces of a ruined and abandoned homeland, have by hard toil built villages and towns, planted gardens and established factories." The problems of the old-timer immigrant, in other words, are mainly seen as fighting nature and fighting the enemy.

This glorified and one-sided picture of the "old" immigration is partly incorrect and is somewhat harmful. The youth who learned to idealize the sacrificing heroism of the "old immigrants" sees in the new immigration, and especially in its Oriental segment, a weak element and a second-rate human material. This attitude of superiority can be illustrated by a statement made by an Israeli adolescent recently:

> We (the old-timers) have built the country, and they (the new immigrants) are coming to enjoy it. . . . We have to explain to them that it is their task to build the country exactly as we did. . . . In case they find it difficult to understand, we will have to force them. (C1:91)

This statement is characteristic of a youth who lacks the basic understanding of the problems of adjustment of the immigrants to Israel in the past and at the present. Literature has an important part to play in sensitizing students to these problems.

The era of the "old immigration" has in it not only lights and successes, but also shadows and failures—such as the demoralizing effects of the Rothschild philanthropy, conflicts between workers and farmers, desertion of the country, and lack of readiness to change from an urban to a rural way of living.

The era is characterized not only by the immigrant's struggle with nature but also by man's struggle with himself and his fellow men, and by his search for status and a place under the sun.

There is a need for a new type of literature which portrays not only the one-track-minded "elite" of pioneers, but also the complexity of the problems of the "common man." Maletz's novel *Bamaagalot* (M3) is an excellent illustration of this type of literature; it is one of the first (and one of the few) attempts to describe the life of a non-pioneering-spirited man in a pioneering group.

Literature should emphasize the basic differences in the socio-psychological aims and problems of the old and the new immigrants. Among the good things that new immigrants are grateful for in Israel, which might be rich material for literature, are political and religious freedom, educational opportunities, greater earning capacity, and hope for a better future.

There are bad things, too, however, in the new environment, especially for the Oriental segment of the new immigration. The major bad things are spiritual displacement, community disintegration, some lack of acceptance by "old stock" Israelis which often amounts to a definite prejudice, lowering of status, and conflicts between parents and children.

These problems were hardly known to the old Ashkenazi immigrant. The old Ashkenazi immigration was, however, and the new Ashkenazi immigration is, faced by socio-economic difficulties. The old Oriental immigrant was, and the new Oriental immigrant is, faced by a cultural crisis. (P1)

Modern Israeli literature should stress and analyze these interpersonal problems of people of different ethnic, socio-economic, and age groups. The whole area of relationships between Oriental and Ashkenazi persons, young and adult, is entirely untouched in Israeli fiction, and calls for the pen of a novelist. A personal-oriented, rather than a task-oriented, literature will help students in getting more insight into the experiences and feelings of people different from themselves.

There is a need for scientific analysis of the ethnic problem, written in non-technical language and adapted to the level of understanding of children. (Excellent examples of this type of literature are the following American studies: Powdermaker's *Probing Our Prejudices* (P6), Benedict's *In Henry's Backyard* (B5), Jaworski's *Becoming American* (J1).) Such reading materials might well have, at the ends of chapters, suggested discussion topics, trips, surveys, interviews, role-playing activities, reading, or use of resource people, which will help the teacher in making the readings more meaningful. Discussion of such books can serve, in addition, to break down stereotypes about rich and poor people, hard workers and shiftless people, laborers and owners.

> Contrasts must be drawn and questions must be raised in such a way that we sharpen the idea that many types of behavior are not characteristic of certain racial and cultural groups, but are outgrowths of economic privileges or deprivation. Generalizations must be made so that the effects of ways of life upon expectations and motivations is clear. (T4:9)

The study of nutrition. "Breaking bread" together can be deeply meaningful. Eating the food of another ethnic group carries with it a sharing and closeness in which attitudes are bound together inextricably. It can link the school and the home and often bring together parent groups that otherwise might never meet.

Favorite recipes supplied by mothers can be tried out at school; and mothers might come to school and prepare dishes for a home economics class, or for a party of pupils and their parents. In these activities the Oriental student has an opportunity to see his mother in a new role. She is a resource person who helps to enrich school living.

Many Oriental mothers, being inarticulate and shy, find it difficult to participate in discussion groups or any other activity which calls for verbal skill. Serving and participating in school life through cooking, sewing, or arts and crafts activities can help such parents overcome their initial resistance and insecurity.

An interesting topic of study is the nutritional habits of the various ethnic groups. Our previous analysis of this topic showed serious deficiencies in the diet of both the Ashkenazi and the Oriental groups. The Sloan experiment in America (O2) shows that the school can play a major role in improving the diet habits of children and of their communities.

The study of music. Musical activities are an effective means of building pleasant associations, friendliness, and intergroup understanding.

In recent years the music of the Oriental Jews has become very popular. Israeli music, looking for an original style, is coming increasingly under the sway of and is influenced more and more by the Oriental music. Oriental songs are taught at school and are sung by the children of the two communities. Seldom, however, is the Oriental character and background of these songs stressed by the teacher. Music expresses the spirit and character of groups in a way that the printed word alone can never equal. Analysis and discussion of these songs will help students understand the mentality, aspirations, and way of life of the Orientals in the past and in the present. (K3)

For instance, it is interesting to compare the content and style of Oriental music with modern Ashkenazi music composed in Israel or as a result of the Zionist movement in Europe. The overwhelming majority of the latter is permeated with the Zionist task spirit. Its "marching melody" sings of the mobilized pioneer who conquers the desert or serves his nation. In contrast to this, the Oriental music is personal-oriented. The individual is seen in his ordinary life activities. The Oriental sings about love, children, birth, death, food, work, and prayers, without putting them in a national context.

Music is also an effective means through which adults of various ethnic origins can be brought to the school—to share their songs and culture with other adults and students.

The study of general science. The general science course affords an opportunity to study the problems of the influence of heredity and environment. Some of the problems to be raised are these: Are there genetic or physiological causes for basic ethnic personality differences? Is environment a factor in the formation of personality? If you live in a room with six other people, would this tend to make your personality different from that of a person who has had a private room in a large house? Does the culture in which one lives influence the values on which his behavior is based? (V1)

In study of the meaning of the scientific method, the stress should be put on solutions of problems through fact-finding procedures in contrast to opinions based on propaganda, rumors, or stereotyped forms of thinking.

Teacher Education

The individual teacher may feel powerless in facing the complexity and severity of the ethnic problem and think that any contribution he might make toward the improvement of intergroup relations would be all but negligible. However, seeing the public school as a strategic institution for the improvement of intergroup relations will help teachers place a higher estimate upon their own value and potential influence. The public school system is the essential training ground for a democratic society. It can give children of various ethnic and socio-economic origins and political ideologies a chance to interact with and learn from one another.

The teacher will utilize the strategic position of the school only if he is aware of the need for intergroup education and only if he is equipped with tools to handle intergroup problems.

The following discussion attempts to outline some basic principles for a teacher education program in the area of intergroup education.

AWARENESS OF THE PROBLEM

There is a need for a program which will sensitize the teacher to the existence of a growing ethnic problem in the country, and which will analyze the socio-psychological factors underlying this problem.

The teacher should be helped to relate the theoretical analysis of the ethnic problem in the country as a whole to his own community. He should learn to analyze the patterns of group relations and the systems of values of the different groups in his community and in his own school, and learn to identify any symptoms of prejudice or other ethnic barriers.

A careful study of the school system will be required for any program which is to lead to recognition and understanding of the impact of the present administrative and curricular principles of the school system on the ethnic problem.

A most important and difficult task is to help the teacher recognize and identify attitudes of prejudice in himself. Even the most liberal of us have hidden prejudices. Despite the most fervent protestations of our belief in the dignity and rights of the individual, we convey disrespect to some groups, and to some individuals *as members of groups,* with a shrug of the shoulder or a tone of voice. The teacher should be helped to approach the minority-group, lower-class, or low-intelligence student in a more objective way.

AN APPROACH TO INTERGROUP EDUCATION

Recognizing the need for intergroup education and being able to identify intergroup problems is an important step. Often, however, good will is vague and inarticulate. The teacher education program should help teachers clarify the major objectives of and approaches to intergroup education.

A study of intergroup programs in American schools shows that teachers differ radically in their theories of how to achieve intergroup unity. According to some of these theories,

> The problem of minorities will be solved if we as teachers pretend they do not exist or if we teach that minorities are quaint and interesting; or if we emphasize that we are all alike under our skins; or if we build secure children; or if we provide first hand contact with minorities; or if we change the minorities to make them more like the predominating group. (S8:x)

A thorough analysis of the various approaches to intergroup education, identifying their merits and possible weaknesses (E1, V2), will help the teacher in building a constructive theory and approach for his specific situation.

Teachers should be helped to see intergroup education in the broader context of modern education and to understand it as an integral part of the need for the democratization of the school.

CURRICULAR PLANS AND MATERIALS

Understanding the theory of intergroup education is very essential for teachers, but it is not enough. To know theory and objectives and yet have no handles for taking hold in one's own situation can lead only to frustration and usually does not result in improved school practices. It is extremely important that tentative, but specific and detailed, curricular plans be elaborated. It is assumed that the teacher who is well versed in the theory and spirit of intergroup education will not be rigid in adapting these tentative plans to his particular classroom.

Curricular plans are conceived broadly here. Some illustrations are plans for (1) systematic units on the important concepts in intergroup unity suited to a specific grade level, (2) ways in which intergroup problems may be integrated into other topics, (3) writing stories or textbooks to promote understanding of human conflicts, (4) setting up criteria for the analysis of specific school situations, and (5) working with parents.

There is an almost infinite variety of concrete work which needs to be done if a program of intergroup education is to be furthered in the school. The teacher educator should realize that it is these specific and concrete problems which bother the teachers in the schools. A sound teacher education program based on the daily concerns of teachers will help them see these problems in a broader theoretical context and will result in integrating practical suggestions with broad generalizations.

Instructional materials and plans are the avenues through which the theory and basic concepts of intergroup education can be translated into the language of constructive classroom practices.

PRE-SERVICE AND IN-SERVICE EDUCATION

Intergroup education is the business of both pre- and in-service education of teachers. It is difficult to see how an effective program of intergroup education could be achieved without the teacher training institution taking the lead in preparing teachers for this task. In addition to a good background in the theory of intergroup education, the student teacher should get actual experience in intergroup living and practice in working at school and in the community on these problems.

At present the education of teachers (especially the work of the teacher training institutions) is confined mainly to pre-service education. The teacher on the job is faced daily with problems which are essentially ethnic group problems even though he may not recognize them as such; and he needs help and guidance.

Starting with an immediate concern of teachers and with a problem of practical value in a given school or community is a most promising approach in getting the involvement and interest of teachers, and in changing classroom practices.

Extension courses, teachers' meetings, development of curriculum centers, demonstration schools, inter-school visitation, supervision, workshops, and action-research projects can be utilized in preparing and helping teachers to work on intergroup problems. The last two methods will be discussed briefly here.

Workshops. Teachers apply to their classrooms not only *what* they were taught, but also *how* they were taught. The workshop is an opportunity not only to learn about principles of modern education, but also to experience and practice them.

Most workshops expect their participants to come with some practical project in mind to work on. The emphasis on working on an immediate concern of teachers tends to bridge the gap between theory and practice. It does away with mastering ideas in a vacuum, and emphasizes the practical application of knowledge. No wonder that Dewey considers the workshop a uniquely valuable application of the principles of modern education. In a recommendation of Kelley's book *The Workshop Way of Learning,* he says this:

> After familiarizing myself with the activities initiated and conducted by the workshop as here described, I have concluded that it supplies the missing and much needed factor in development of the theory of progressive education. For it applies to the training of teachers the principles that have been set forth as applicable to and in the education of those under instruction. (K2)

The teacher education program in Israel will find the workshop way of learning a most suitable method for developing leadership in intergroup education. (T3)

Action Research. The preparation of teachers for intergroup work will usually require a basic change in their attitudes and practices. One way of attempting to introduce such changes may be through the acquisition of facts and information about intergroup relations in Israel. Although factual familiarity with the situation is necessary, it is questionable whether a linear relationship between knowledge and change exists. For most people, and especially for teachers who are a product of formal schooling, it is easy to be satisfied with the type of education which is passed to them by authorities. Passive absorption of information and ideas, however, cannot by itself be expected to change attitudes and practices.

The action research movement believes that for the practitioner and the policy-maker, active involvement in a study of an urgent problem is more influential in changing practices than the study of finished reports of others. Corey says:

> I have lost much of the faith I once had in the consequences of asking only the professional educational investigator to study the schools and to recommend what they should do. Incorporating these recommendations into the behavior patterns of practitioners involves some problems that so far have been insoluble. . . . Most of the study of what should be kept in the schools and what should go and what should be added must be done in hundreds of thousands of classrooms. . . . The studies must be undertaken by those who may have to change the way they do things as a result of the studies. Our schools cannot keep up with the life they are supposed to sustain and improve unless teachers, pupils, supervisors, administrators, and school patrons continuously examine what they are doing. Singly and in groups, they must use their imaginations creatively and constructively to identify the practices that must be changed to meet the needs and demands of modern life, courageously try out those practices that give better promise, and methodically and systematically gather evidence to test their worth. (C3:viii)

The present Israeli society is undergoing continuous and profound change. Nothing is more needful in a rapidly changing society than flexibility and a spirit of experimentation. In order to meet the changing needs of our society, educators have to be equipped with the ability to question the old and try out the new ideas.

The ethnic relations in Israel present educational problems for which there are no immediate and ready-made answers. Educators are bewildered and apprehensive. The old methods of education do not apply, but new ways are as yet unknown. This situation is paralyzing and defeating. It is paralyzing mainly because our educators have not been trained in experimentation. If a teacher can only dare to try out her ideas and evaluate them objectively, she may not only save herself from pessimism, but also find constructive ways of improving education.

There is need for the creation of an institute of action research, attached to the Board of Education or to the Hebrew University, which will help educators and laymen to identify ethnic problems in the classroom, school, and community, and to experiment with various approaches to their solution.

RECRUITING ORIENTAL TEACHERS

The teacher with a background similar to that of his students has the best chance of understanding them, knowing their motivations and daily experiences, and dealing with their parents. Teachers should be selected from a wide range of socio-economic classes and ethnic groups.

Some Oriental youth see the attainment of a teaching position as a promotion in their socio-economic status. (M4) However, the lack of free secondary education makes this attainment impossible for the majority of these young people. Helping Oriental youth become teachers calls for a long-range program. The recruiting processes should start in the elementary school by helping graduates of Oriental origin get a high school education and during these high school years providing for them a variety of experiences in working with children.

The possibilities of coordinating these efforts with the few *free* municipal high schools, and with the military service, should be explored.

Summary

Decent relationships between the students of the two ethnic groups cannot be achieved in an authoritarian school. Where frustration, bickering, or boredom reigns over pupils' lives, democratic human relations wither. Where youngsters belong, have an active role, and are respected as individuals, healthy ethnic group attitudes can be created. A classroom program composed of activities involving a high degree of interaction is conducive to intergroup cooperation.

Plans for homogeneous grouping, which may on the one hand reduce academic failure but will on the other hand intensify ethnic segregation, can be rejected only if the curriculum will provide for a wide range of interests and abilities, and only if the school will accept different kinds and qualities of participation from different pupils.

The suggestion to abolish the defeating policy of non-promotion and establish a policy of continuous progress, and to encourage inter-ethnic participation, will encounter open or hidden resistance unless the public can be convinced that these policies will not lower the academic standards of the schools.

The difficulties of integrating the Ashkenazi and Oriental communities stem not only from ethnic differences but are also rooted in socio-economic conditions. Vocational education can play an important role in widening the channels of socio-economic mobility. Vocational information, a variety of work experiences in the community, psychotechnical guidance, vocational schools and centers, cooperative projects with industry and business, cooperation with labor and management, child labor and apprenticeship laws, are some of the avenues through which educators can help both Oriental and Ashkenazi students become skilled and intelligent workers.

Teachers must aim at developing desirable intergroup attitudes and relationships through a direct program based on the study of ethnic group problems. This direct program should: (1) Permeate every aspect of the curriculum rather than become a new subject. (2) Utilize many kinds of activities rather than rely upon a single approach. (3) Be realistic rather than "romantic." (4) Help the minority group member accept his group belonging. (5) Inspire the students with readiness to help the less fortunate. (6) Study the intergroup problems of the school and the community.

The following areas and subjects can be fruitfully explored for their special possibilities as grounds for the study of intergroup problems: The community, the family, the holidays, religion, history, geography, literature, nutrition, music, and science.

Seeing the public school as a strategic institution for the improvement of intergroup relations will help teachers place a higher estimate upon their own value and potential influence as community leaders. It is the task of the teacher education program to arouse the teacher to exploit this strategic position. The teacher education program has to: (1) Help teachers become aware of manifestations of ethnic tension in the school and in the community. (2) Encourage teachers to accept responsibility for helping school and community members examine their own prejudices. (3) Build a theory of intergroup education as an integral part of modern education. (4) Equip the teacher with skill in handling intergroup problems. (5) Emphasize the need for both pre-service and in-service training in intergroup education. (6) Recruit Oriental teachers.

Part Five

SUMMARY

XI

Summary

THE CONTACT BETWEEN WESTERN AND ORIENTAL CIVILIZA-
tions has brought with it to the Orient not only technical advancement
and progress, but also tensions and frustrations. Factors often cited as
underlying these tensions are Western imperialism, attitudes of white
supremacy, and policies of discrimination. There is another factor,
however, which is an important as the above, if not more important.
That is, cultural contact alone between West and East is often a source
of disintegration in the culture of the Orientals. A striking example of
this cultural impact exists in South African tribal life. Paton, describing the disintegration of South African tribal life and the crime and
delinquency which disfigure African urban life as a result, says: "A
whole nation has been rocked to its foundations. It was struck by the
giant forces of Western civilization, but not with any plan or concert."
(P3:17)

This study is based on the premise that the close contact between the
Ashkenazi Jews—those who came from the West—and the Oriental
Jews—those who came from the Middle East—results in some discontinuity in the Oriental culture. This crisis is manifested in their economic life, ethnic cohesiveness, family life, and education. Contact
with the Ashkenazi group results in a crisis in the relationship of the
Oriental person to his group and to the prevailing norms and values in
the group. It decreases group cohesiveness and it decreases the individual's happiness. Sociologically speaking, we witness a manifestation
of anomie—the lack of a well-organized system of values and norms
which regulates the behavior of the individual and sustains his mental
health. (E6, F7)

The two Jewish groups have diverged in their development. The Ashkenazim have a secular conception of Jewish nationality and a rejection of the Jewish life of the Diaspora. Consequently, their main objective in coming to Israel was social and cultural reconstruction. This positive predisposition for change partly explains why in spite of radical change in value system, ego-ideals, occupational structure, language, and communal and family relations, conditions of anomie were not created in the Ashkenazi culture. (E8)

Coming from the feudal Arab countries, the Oriental Jew has never learned to believe in the power of the individual to change and to determine his own fate. In other words, the Oriental is characterized by a low predisposition toward change—a disadvantage in Israel, where he met with the Ashkenazi way of life.

For instance, in the area of economy the difficulties of the Orientals stem not only from their poverty (they are in general the lower class in Israel) but also from the disruption of their previous economic structure. This discontinuity is manifested in the transition from an autarchical to a specialized and impersonal economy, in which the Oriental has lost his status as an independent artisan and has become an unskilled employee. (E6) It is also manifested in the discontinuity of the family's guiding function in vocational and economic preparation, and in the lowering of the status of the family head. (Y5)

The lower economic status of the Orientals, the discontinuity of their previous economic structure, and the difference in socio-economic milieu between them and the Ashkenazim produce, in the Oriental, feelings of frustration, self-depreciation, and discrimination.

Other dangers to the mental health of the Oriental result from the dissolution of the previous pattern of relationship between the Oriental groups and their leaders, and from the resulting isolation and individuation. (E7) Applying Fromm's analysis of negative freedom, I can say that the Oriental "has been freed from traditional authorities and has become an individual, but at the same time he has become isolated, powerless . . . this state undermines his self, weakens and frightens him." (F11)

The present stage of anomie has especially detrimental effects on the mental health of the Oriental youth. In many cases, it creates a disintegrated and marginal person of uncertain belongingness. This stage of marginality and rootlessness sometimes leads to maladjustive and antisocial behavior. (F5) It is likely, moreover, that the adjustment of the second-generation Orientals will not be smoother, but on the contrary may even be more difficult.

The Oriental child is unable to identify with his parents, who deviate from the social norms of the dominant Ashkenazi culture. On the other hand, he himself finds it difficult to become thoroughly acquainted with the Ashkenazi way of life, mainly because he does not have sufficient opportunities for association with the Ashkenazim in close primary groups.

I have analyzed some of the major social institutions in terms of their ethnic composition and in terms of the role the Oriental youth plays in them. Some of these institutions are the youth movement, the club, the coffeehouse, and the Army. I found that in spite of an absence of any policy of segregation, the lack of understanding of the importance of inter-ethnic association results in some *de facto* segregation. The major effects of this segregation are two: (1) intensification of the conditions of anomie in which the Oriental youth lives, and (2) the development of attitudes of prejudice.

The educational authorities, too, have failed to consider the importance of inter-ethnic association in the school; and the result is some segregation based on a policy of "gentlemen's agreement." One may summarize the status of the average Oriental pupil by saying that he is a problem child in the school.

The many efforts of the school to help the Oriental child and his community are hampered by a policy of non-promotion, which means that the average Oriental pupil does not succeed in graduating from the elementary school. (E13, O1)

Three major causes for the failure and low achievement of the Oriental pupil were examined: intelligence, social class, and the present curriculum.

1. The claim that low intelligence is responsible for the failure of the Oriental pupil is only partly valid. The number of Orientals who fail at school is much higher than their number in the low-intelligence group. The present intelligence tests, moreover, are culturally biased so as to discriminate against the Oriental.

2. Behind the failure of the Oriental pupil lies the social system. In contrast to the middle-class Ashkenazi child, the lower-class Oriental is not culturally motivated to achieve academic success. He is not

helped in his homework and he is not trained in the specific culture emphasized by the academic school. He often brings with him to school expectations with regard to behavior which are at variance with the school expectations. In brief, the problem of the Oriental pupil is being a lower-class child in a middle-class school.

3. The present academic curriculum is the major factor in the failure of the Oriental pupil. Its content and method of presentation tend to polarize the school into two groups: the successful (mainly Ashkenazi) and the unsuccessful (mainly Oriental).

The effects of the subject curriculum make the school an instrument for creating the very inequalities it was designed to prevent. Instead of becoming the means for raising the socio-economic standard of living of the Oriental community and eliminating ethnic and class distinctions, the school often perpetuates their low economic status and solidifies ethnic barriers, increasing insecurity, maladjustment, and inferiority feeling among the Orientals.

The results of the analysis of the culture contact in Israel point to three major tasks confronting the school: (1) to help raise the socio-economic standard of living of the Oriental, (2) to alleviate the conditions of anomie in the Oriental community, the consequent tensions in the family, and the marginality among the youth, and (3) to bring the people and especially the youth of the two communities into participation on an equal basis, in order that they may live in close association and gradually construct a new culture based on the values of both communities.

In order to achieve these goals three interrelated steps were outlined, in some detail, in Chapter X: (1) the democratization of the school curriculum and organization, (2) vocational education, and (3) the direct study of intergroup problems as a part of the school program.

The many curricular suggestions analyzed in the previous chapter stress one major point: The improvement of ethnic group relations is an integral part of building an atmosphere of better human relations throughout the school. Both in the school and in the country as a whole, the aim should be to build a culture as fruitfully oriented to personal fulfillment as to national goals.

It is customary in my culture to conclude a work such as this by interpreting a verse or proverb. Twenty years ago, the Israeli poet

Tchernikhovsky wrote a poem called "The Ingathering of the Exiles." (T9:51) One statement from this poem is now a byword:

> We were united before your mountains,
> Brother to brother, hand to hand.

The Ashkenazim have met their Oriental brothers with economic assistance, and with some patronizing, perhaps fatherly, love. They have failed, however, to extend to them the brotherly hand of equal respect. That this brotherly hand may be extended is the hope to which my study is dedicated.

Bibliography

(*The starred references are Hebrew publications. Passages quoted from these, in the text, were translated by the author.*)

A1 ALBERTY, HAROLD. *Reorganizing the High School Curriculum.* New York: The Macmillan Company, 1950.

A2 ASSOCIATION FOR SUPERVISION AND CURRICULUM DEVELOPMENT. *Growing Up in an Anxious Age.* Washington: National Education Association, 1952.

A3 ASSOCIATION OF ASSISTANT SUPERINTENDENTS. *Policies and Practices Affecting Elementary Schools.* New York City Board of Education, 1952.

*A4 AVIZEMER, S. "An Unsolved Problem." *Hapoel Hatzair,* April 29, 1952.

*A5 AVNON, D. "New Developments in Psychology." *Hakhinuch,* No. 3, 1949.

B1 BACHI, R. *Inquiring into Poverty and Malnutrition Among the Jews of Jerusalem.* Jerusalem: Hadassa Emergency Committee, 1943.

*B2 ———. *The Hebrew Pupil in Jerusalem.* Jerusalem: The Szold Foundation, 1944.

*B3 BAKALIAR, S. "A Comparative Analysis of Non-Verbal Intelligence Tests." *Hakhinuch,* No. 2, 1951.

*B4 ———. "Characteristics of Yemenite Youth." *Hakhinuch,* No. 3, 1949.

B5 BENEDICT, R. *In Henry's Backyard.* New York: Henry Schuman, 1948.

B6 BOARD OF EDUCATION, NEW YORK CITY. *Unity through Understanding.* Curriculum Bulletin No. 4, 1945.

B7 BOGARDUS, S. "The Measurement of Social Distance" in T. Newcomb's *Readings in Social Psychology.* New York: Henry Holt and Company, 1947.

*B8 BRACHIAHU. "Mental Hygiene Problems in Our Schools." *Hakhinuch,* No. 1, 1952.

B9 BRAMELD, T. *Minority Problems in the Public School.* New York: Harper and Brothers, 1944.

*B10 BRILL, M. "Retarded and Non-Promoted Pupils." *Hakhinuch,* 1938.

B11 ———. *The School Attendance of Jewish Children in Jerusalem.* Jerusalem: The Hebrew University, 1941.

*C1 CAZENELSON'S SEMINARY. *Discussions,* Vol. 1. Tel Aviv: Mapai, 1951.

*C2 CALFON, A. "Toward Mutual Assimilation." *Davar,* Aug. 21, 1952.

C3 COREY, S. *Action Research to Improve School Practices.* New York: Bureau of Publications, Teachers College, Columbia University, 1953.

C4 CYDEROVITCH, G. *The Living Standards of the Jewish Community at the End of the World War.* Jerusalem: The Economic Research Institute of the Jewish Agency, Vol. X, No. 2, 1946.

D1 DAVIS, A. and HAVIGHURST, J. *Father of the Man.* Boston: Houghton Mifflin Company, 1947.

D2 DAVIS, A. "Socialization and Adolescent Personality" in T. Newcomb (ed.), *Readings in Social Psychology.* New York: Henry Holt and Company, 1947.

D3 ———. *Social Class Influences Upon Learning.* Cambridge, Mass.: Harvard University Press, 1951.

D4 DEWEY, J. *Experience and Education.* New York: The Macmillan Company, 1938.

*D5 DINABURG, B. Z. "The Task of Education." *Hed-Hakhinuch,* 2.27.52.

*D6 DUSHKIN, A. and BRILL, M. "To What Extent Are Our Children Educated?" *Magness Book,* 1938.

E1 EDMAN, M. *Promising Practices in Intergroup Education.* New York: Bureau of Intercultural Education, 1947.

E2 EELLS, K. and ASSOCIATES. *Intelligence and Cultural Differences.* Chicago: University of Chicago Press, 1951. Copyright 1951 by The University of Chicago.

E3 EFRON, D. "Gestural Behavior and Social Setting" in T. Newcomb (ed.), *Readings in Social Psychology.* New York: Henry Holt and Company, 1947.

*E4 EISENSTADT, S. N. *Absorption of Immigrants in Israel.* Jerusalem: The Hebrew University, 1952.

E5 ———. *Absorption of Immigrants in Israel* (English Summary). Jerusalem: The Hebrew University, 1952.

*E6 ———. *An Introduction to the Sociological Structure of Oriental Jewry.* Jerusalem: The Szold Foundation, 1948.

E7 ———. "The Role of Elite and Primary Groups in the Absorption of New Immigrants in Israel." *The American Journal of Sociology,* Vol. LVII, No. 3, November, 1951.

E8 ———. "The Social Development of Israel." *Middle Eastern Affairs,* Vol. II, No. 5, 1951.

E9 ———. "The Sociological Structure of the Jewish Community in Palestine." *Jewish Social Studies,* Vol. X, No. 1, 1948.

E10 ELSBREE, W. and McNALLY, H. *Elementary School Administration and Supervision.* New York: American Book Company, 1951.

E11 ELSBREE, W. "Promotion Policies in the Elementary School." *Teachers College Record,* Vol. 48, No. 7, April, 1947.

*E12 ENOCH, D. "Elementary School Graduates in Tel Aviv." *Megamot,* Vol. IV, No. 1, 1952.

*E13 ———. "Non-Promotion in Elementary Schools in Tel Aviv." *Megamot,* Vol. II, No. 1, 1950.

E14 ERICKSON, E. *Childhood and Society.* New York: W. W. Norton and Company, 1950.

E15 ERICSON, M. "Social Status and Child Rearing Practices" in T. Newcomb (ed.), *Readings in Social Psychology*. New York: Henry Holt and Company, 1947.

F1 FARIS, R. "Ecological Factors in Human Behavior" in *Personality and the Behavior Disorders*, Vol. II (J. McV. Hunt, Editor). Copyright 1944 by The Ronald Press Company, New York.

*F2 FEITELSON, D. "Patterns of Early Education Among the Kurds." *Megamot*, Vol. V, No. 2, 1954.

F3 FRANKENSTEIN, C. (ed.). *Between Past and Future*. Jerusalem: The Szold Foundation, 1953.

*F4 ———. "Notes and Comments." *Megamot*, Vol. I, No. 2, 1950.

*F5 ———. "Notes and Comments." *Megamot*, Vol. III, No. 3, 1952.

*F6 ———. "The Psychological Approach to the Problem of Ethnic Differences." *Megamot*, Vol. III, No. 2, 1952.

*F7 ———. *Youth-Waywardness*. Jerusalem, The Szold Foundation, 1947.

*F8 ———. "Youth Aliyah and the Education of Young Immigrants." *Megamot*, Vol. IV, No. 3, 1953.

*F9 ———. "Waywardness Among the Youth in Jerusalem." *Hakhinuch*, No. 1, 1938.

*F10 FROID, I. "Visiting Immigrants' Settlements." *Tlamim*, No. 151, Nov., 1952.

F11 FROMM, E. *Escape from Freedom*. New York: Rinehart and Company, 1941.

*F12 FUAH, O. "The Influence of Ethnic and Socio-Economic Origin on the Interrelationships Among Young Children." *Hakhinuch*, Sept., 1947.

*G1 GELBLUM, A. "The Truth About Human Material." *Haaretz*, April 22, 1949.

*G2 GOITINE, S. "Jewish Education in Yemen." *Megamot*, Vol. II, No. 2, 1951.

*G3 GROSS, Y. "Ethnic Differences or Social Change." *Megamot*, Vol. III, No. 2, 1952.

G4 GOUGH, H. "Children's Ethnic Attitudes." *Child Development*, 21, 1950.

*H1 HAARETZ. "The Problem of the Tribes and Their Integration." *Haaretz*, April 15, 1952.

H2 HARMAN, Z. "The Assimilation of Immigrants into Israel." *The Middle East Journal*, Vol. V, No. 3, 1951.

H3 HARRIS, D. "Children's Ethnic Attitudes." *Child Development*, 21, 1950.

H4 HEATON, M. *Feelings Are Facts*. New York: National Conference of Christians and Jews, 1952.

H5 HODGES, N. *Community Service in the Dalton School*. New York: The Dalton School, 1949.

H6 HOLLINGSHEAD, A. *Elmtown's Youth*. New York, John Wiley and Sons, 1949.

H7 HOROWITZ, E. "The Development of Attitudes Toward Negroes." *Archives of Psychology*, No. 194, 1936.

*I1 INSTITUTE OF APPLIED SOCIAL RESEARCH. *Adjustment to Work*. Tel Aviv: Labor Ministry, 1950.

*I2 ———. *The Public's Opinion on Foreign Language Newspapers*. Jerusalem: The Institute, 1949.

*I3 ISRAELI HIGH SCHOOL ASSOCIATION. *High School Problems*. Jerusalem: The Association, 1953.

J1   JAWORSKI, I. *Becoming American.* New York: Harper and Brothers, 1950.

J2   JENNINGS, H. *Sociometry in Group Relations.* Washington: American Council on Education, 1948.

*J3   JEWISH AGENCY. *The Economic Development of Jerusalem.* Jerusalem: Statistical Department, 1947.

K1   KELLEY, E. *Education for What Is Real.* New York: Harper and Brothers, 1947.

K2   ———. *The Workshop Way of Learning.* New York: Harper and Brothers, 1951.

*K3   KIWI-GERSHON, E. "The Musicians of the Orient." *Edoth,* July, 1946.

K4   KLINEBERG, O. *Negro Intelligence and Selective Migration.* New York: Columbia University Press, 1935.

K5   KLUCKHOHN, C. and ASSOC. "American Culture" in L. Bryson (ed.), *Conflicts of Power in Modern Culture.* New York: Harper and Brothers, 1947.

K6   KOCH, H. "The Social Distance Between Certain Racial Groups of American School Children." *Journal of Genetic Psychology,* No. 68, 1946.

*K7   KOREN, I. *The Settling of the Immigrants in 1949–50.* Tel Aviv: The Workers' Union, 1951.

K8   KRECH, D. and ASSOC. *Theory and Problems of Social Psychology.* New York: McGraw-Hill Book Company, 1948.

*K9   KRIVINE, D. "Working Children." *Megamot,* Vol. IV, No. 3, 1953.

*L1   LEVIN, D. "The Mission of the Teacher." *Shviley-Hakhinuch,* No. 1, Nov., 1952.

*L2   LEVINTON, Y. "The Story of the General School in Yazur." *Shviley-Hakhinuch,* No. 3, May, 1950.

L3   LEWIN, K. "Dynamics of Group Action." *Educational Leadership,* January, 1944.

L4   ———. "Group Decision and Social Change" in T. Newcomb (ed.), *Readings in Social Psychology.* New York: Henry Holt and Company, 1947.

L5   ———. *Resolving Social Conflicts.* New York: Harper and Brothers, 1948.

*L6   LITWAK, Y. "Absorption of Immigrant Youth from North Africa." *Megamot,* Vol. IV, No. 4, 1953.

M1   MACMULL, A. "The Indian Jewry in Israel." *Jerusalem Post,* May 2, 1952.

*M2   MAIMON, J. "Voluntary Teachers in Immigrant Camps." *Megamot,* Vol. IV, No. 1, 1952.

*M3   MALETZ, Y. *Bamaagalot.* Tel Aviv: Am-Oved, 1943.

*M4   MALINOVSKY, L. and DAUBER, M. *The Vocational Interests of Urban Youth.* Jerusalem: The Szold Foundation, No. 31, 1947.

M5   MERTON, R. "Social Structure and Anomie." *American Sociological Review,* Vol. III, 1938.

N1   NADAD, A. *Reeducation of Wayward Youth.* Jerusalem: The Szold Foundation, No. 25, 1946.

N2   NEWCOMB, T. *Social Psychology.* Copyright 1950 by The Dryden Press, Inc., New York. Quoted matter reprinted by special permission.

*O1   OESTEREICHER, G. *Early School Leaving in Jerusalem.* Jerusalem: The Szold Foundation, 1948.

O2   OLSON, C. *Learn and Live.* New York: Sloan Foundation, 1946.

O3   ORGANIZATION OF YEMENITE JEWS. *The Yemenite Jews in the State of Israel.* Tel Aviv: The Organization, 1950.

*O4 ORMIAN, H. "Adolescent Types in Israel" in Cazenelson's Seminary, *The Israeli Youth.* Tel Aviv: Mapai, 1951.

*O5 ORNY, Y. "Parents and Sons in the Immigrant Settlements." *Hed-Hakhinuch,* July 17, 1951.

*O6 ORTAR, G. "Differences in the Structure of Intelligence." *Megamot,* Vol. IV, No. 2, 1953.

*O7 ORTAR, G. and FRANKENSTEIN, C. "How to Develop Abstract Thinking in Immigrant Children from Oriental Countries." *Megamot,* Vol. II, No. 4, 1951.

P1   PATAI, R. *Israel Between East and West.* Philadelphia: Jewish Publication Society, 1953.

P2   ———. "On Cultural Contact and Its Working in Modern Palestine." *American Anthropologist,* Vol. 49, No. 4, 1947.

P3   PATON, A. *South Africa Today.* Public Affairs Pamphlet No. 175, 1951.

P4   PHILADELPHIA PUBLIC SCHOOLS. *Toward Social Competence.* School District of Philadelphia, 1950.

*P5 POLACK, A. *The Hebrew Population at the End of the War.* Merhavia: Workers' Library, 1945.

P6   POWDERMAKER, H. *Probing Our Prejudices.* New York: Harper and Brothers, 1944.

R1   RABINOWITZ, B. "Hygiene, Education and Nutrition among Kurdish, Persian and Ashkenazi Jews in Jerusalem." Jerusalem: *Social Studies,* Vol. 1, 1948.

R2   RADKE, M. and ASSOC. "Social Perceptions and Attitudes of Children." *Genetic Psychology Monographs,* No. 40, 1949.

*R3 RIEGER, E. *Hebrew Education in Palestine.* Tel Aviv: Dvir, 1940.

*R4 RIEGER, H. "Some Aspects of the Acculturation of Young Yemenite Immigrants." *Megamot,* Vol. III, No. 3, 1952.

*R5 ROBINSON, S. "On Citizenship Education." *Megamot,* Vol. IV, No. 3, 1953.

*R6 ROTENSHTRIECH, N. "Range and Altitude." *Hadoar,* Feb. 20, 1953.

*S1 SAPIR, R. "A Home." *Megamot,* Vol. III, No. 1, 1951.

S2   SCHECTMAN, J. "Beware of Color Prejudice." *Congress Weekly,* Vol. 19, No. 14, 4.7.52.

*S3 SHANAN, Y. "Teaching Maladjusted Children." *Megamot,* Vol. III, No. 2, 1952.

*S4 SHUR, F. "Causes of Scholastic Failure in First Graders." *Megamot,* Vol. IV, No. 1, October, 1952, and No. 2, January, 1953.

*S5 SIMON, A. "The Structure of Elementary Education in an Immigrant Town." *Megamot,* Vol. IV, No. 4, 1953.

*S6 SIMON, E. "On the Double Meaning of the Concept of Primitivity." *Megamot,* Vol. II, No. 3, 1951.

*S7 SNAPIR, I. "Descriptions." *Dvar-Hashavua,* July 24, 1952.

S8   STENDLER, C. and MARTIN, W. *Intergroup Education in Kindergarten-Primary Grades.* New York: The Macmillan Company, 1953. Quoted matter reprinted by permission of The Macmillan Company.

S9   SYRKIN, M. "Oriental Jews in Israel." *Jewish Frontier,* April, 1952.

T1 TABA, H. *Diagnosing Human Relations Needs.* Washington: American Council on Education, 1951.

T2 ———. *Elementary Curriculum in Intergroup Relations.* Washington: American Council on Education, 1950.

T3 ———. *Leadership Training in Intergroup Education.* Washington: American Council on Education, 1953.

T4 ———. *Literature for Human Understanding.* Washington: American Council on Education, 1948.

T5 ———. *With Focus on Human Relations.* Washington: American Council on Education, 1950.

*T6 TAHON, H. "The Orientals in Israel." *Dvar-Hapoelet,* 8.12.46.

*T7 ———. *Thirty Moroccan Families in Old Jerusalem.* Jerusalem: The Szold Foundation, 1948.

*T8 TANNENBAUM, J. "Social Relationships Among New Immigrants." *Hakhinuch,* No. 2, 1951.

*T9 TCHERNIKHOVSKY, S. *Poems.* Jerusalem: Shoken, 1950.

T10 TRAGER, H. and RADKE, M. *They Learn What They Live.* New York: Harper and Brothers, 1952.

T11 TYLER, R. "Can Intelligence Tests Be Used to Predict Educability?" in Eells, K. and Associates, *Intelligence and Cultural Differences.* Chicago: University of Chicago Press, 1951. Copyright 1951 by The University of Chicago.

V1 VAN-TIL, W. *Democracy Demands It.* New York: Harper and Brothers, 1950.

V2 VICKERY, W. *Intercultural Education in American Schools.* New York: Harper and Brothers, 1943.

*W1 WALDSTEIN, D. "Some Characteristics of Israelis of East European Origin." *Hakhinuch,* No. 2, 1953.

W2 WARNER, W. L. and SROLE, L. *The Social System of American Ethnic Groups.* New Haven: Yale University Press, 1946.

W3 WATSON, G. *Action for Unity.* New York: Harper and Brothers, 1947.

*Y1 YESHAYAHU, I. "Changes Among the Yemenites." *Beterem,* Sept., 1947.

Y2 ———. "East and West in the Melting Pot." *Chayenu,* Vol. VIII, No. 4, 1945.

*Y3 ———. *On the Way.* Tel Aviv: The Workers' Union, 1947.

*Y4 ———. "The Problem of Tribes and Their Synthesis." *Hador,* April 9, 1952.

*Y5 ———. *The Yemen Return.* Tel Aviv: From Yemen to Zion, 1945.

Z1 ZRUBAVEL. "The Immigration of Oriental Jewry" in *Problems of the Oriental Jewry.* Jerusalem: The Jewish Agency, 1951.